MW00939529

The Boomer Blues

The Boomer Blues

Dick Caplan

Copyright © 2016 Dick Caplan
All rights reserved.

ISBN-13: 9781532852954
ISBN-10: 1532852959
Library of Congress Control Number: 2016906622
CreateSpace Independent Publishing Platform
North Charleston, South Carolina

To my father, Thomas D. Caplan
His life taught me to live passionately, with compassion for all.
I was twenty-three years old when he died in March of 1974. He
was seventy. As a grown-up, I learned about him from others—
for me, he was a man of few words. In his honor, I have just
written some sixty-eight thousands of them.

Table of Contents

Acknowledgments

BECAUSE THIS BOOK IS A memoir, the people I'd like to acknowledge are my family and a few others I've met and shared some time-stopping moments with during my journey. I thank them all, beginning with my grandparents. They left Russia in the 1890's as young adults; braved the westward journey to the western shores of the Atlantic Ocean; suffered the trip across that ocean; and alone, relocated to a country where their language was not spoken, their religion not welcomed, their holidays and customs not observed—and their family and friends six thousand miles away. They did this knowing they would probably never see their parents, grandparents, relatives, and friends ever again.

My childhood neighborhood offered me a basic New England small-town fifties boyhood. Play was good. A child could roam some. TV cartoons and westerns were fabulous. Disney movies were "supercalifragilisticexpialidocious."

My adolescent years, spent mostly in an out-of-state private high school, were a little too stuffy for me. Thank god for sports. In college I finally found young people I could relate to, drug with, bond with, make music with, get drunk with, experience sex with, test love and life on the road with—and, when time allowed, even learn with. "College," I told everyone, "was a good run."

Back in the fifties, in my neighborhood, there was Skipper, Kathy, Sy, Bruce, Tarn, Laura, and Leila. There was constant play, sports, and, as I got older hand holding and a first kiss. Time went by, and then in high school there was Steve, Greg, Mike, Judy, Margo. In another second, college—and then came David, Paula, Eric, Nardy, Ben, and Chris.

For a while there was one lover; then no lovers; then that same one lover again. Then there was another breakup. Soon all my friends got married. Soon all my friends were divorced. Then all my friends remarried.

After college came Claire. I think I spent more time with her on this journey than anyone else on the planet. I think my dad did, too. She was my dad's secretary since 1948 when he hired her fresh out of high school. He trained her and she came to oversee his businesses and eventually manage his office. Then, when he died, she became my secretary forever. She was/is an efficient, effective, kind, protective, compassionate, competent, stubborn, incredibly loyal woman who also possessed superior human-being skills.

Claire balanced me, focused me, and kept me humble. She, like most of her Depression-era generation, lived by the phrase "waste not, want not." Long before it was fashionable, she recycled and reused with passion.

Sixty-two years after he hired her, she retired from the two of us. She thinks working for us was an even swap. But I'll tell you this: the Caplans got the better deal, hands down. Anyone in my family would tell you that. Anyone who knew or knows her now would tell you that. She personifies the phrase "they don't build them like that anymore."

There were my older sisters. Both of them explained the many mysteries of life to me, patched me up when I hit the inevitable unavoidable bumps in the road, taught me to dance—and, at exactly the right time, revealed that Santa Claus did not really exist; it *was* Mom and Dad all along.

My parents were always there. They nourished me and civilized me. They provided advantages for me whenever there was an opportunity. We were mainly a nuclear family. I suspect much of my extended family in Russia died in either World War I or World War II. .

For the past thirty-three years there is my wife, Karen; our two children, Tom and Samantha; and—over the years—three dogs (Joshua, Spencer, and Clio) and two cats (Binkins and Hillary).

They are and were all so important to me. My words always fall short in expressing my love for everyone. I thank them all. Hugs and kisses all around.

Introduction

IN 1968, I SWITCHED MY college major from engineering to English. I had it in mind to seek a career in writing—creative writing. This book, my first, came into being some forty-three years following the decision to change my major.

This book is an attempt to tell some Caplan family history that took place from the late nineteenth century to the early twenty-first century. It's mostly my own story, and the little I know of my grandparents' and my dad's lives. It also highlights a small, 340-year-old town just north of New Haven, Connecticut. I have come to believe that this old Yankee town, where we lived and I still live, was mostly my father's town—not mine or my grandparents. He lived here his whole life. Except for nine years in my adolescence and early adulthood, I have too. Why did we live here? Circumstance. Both of us lived here by circumstance—different circumstances, of course—but nothing more.

Lastly, the book attempts to blend in a series of late-twentieth-century events that I believe shaped a significant part of the baby boomer generation's (my generation) thoughts, actions, and feelings—certainly my own.

Now, in the early twenty-first century, if I had to say which part of my generation I was speaking for, I believe it would be safe to say I represent the "blue" part of us. Politically, the rhythms and the notions of the "red" contingent have never found their way to my heart or my mind.

If you were to mention "reds" to my father, fifty years ago, he would have thought you were referring to communists. Now "reds" are Republicans.

Politically, my dad was an Independent most of his life. Perhaps his retail food business and his very public role in his small town drove his lack of political connection or affiliation. I do not know. My sisters and I have thought of him as a true Independent. He voted for Roosevelt during the Depression, then later on for Eisenhower—twice. In the sixties, he voted for Kennedy. I imagine he struggled with the same frustrations we all experience today: our politicians, if re-elected often enough, seem to lose much of the common sense they were born with.

These current American reds—Republicans—are certainly not communists, but I worry about some of their group; I believe many of them are getting ready to give up on democracy—or at least the democracy we all knew and cherished. What they have in mind is anyone's guess. It certainly isn't a political party a guy like President Dwight D. Eisenhower would be warmly welcomed in.

The current red politicians seem intent on making changes to laws that will primarily impact the hundreds of thousands of people who have migrated here during the past forty to fifty years (legally and illegally) from Mexico, Central America, South America, Africa, India, the Pacific Rim, China, and Southeast Asia. These people are sometimes called "people of color." Many of these people have children who were born right here in the United States, and who *are* by birthright American citizens—there are millions of them.

The last time that this country attempted to empower people of color, all hell broke loose. Six hundred thousand of us died right on our own soil in a tragic civil war to decide whether black people would be freed or remain slaves of white people.

And one hundred years after the bloody civil war that supposedly freed the black slaves and gave them the same rights as whites, during the 1960's, new laws had to be passed to ensure that people of color had the same freedoms they had supposedly already been given so long ago.

So here are a few words on: <u>authenticity of content</u>. It is a memoir; but except for the stories my own father, my family, and Claire have told me, I can't really vouch for everything else. Many stories have been told to me by Wallingford residents I know and some stories from folks I had never met before.

Lastly and most importantly about my generation: the red and blue among us certainly have significant differences these days. It's practically impossible to agree on what day of the week it is. But in spite of that, and in the spirit of the late sixties, I say, "Peace. Peace to all you red and blue boomers…In fact, peace to everyone!"

Catastrophes Past and Present

A MOMENT AGO, I WAS seventeen years old. It was 1966. If you were to ask me how old my dad was, I'd have told you he was pretty old. You know: slightly thinning hair with a bit of gray, the beginning of an expanded waistline, and tired eyes. He was old, but he was still a handsome man—handsome for sixty-two. I was a gazillion years younger. Then, in a lightning flash moment, it was April of 2011 and I was turning sixty-two! "Magic," I thought to myself as I walked in the woods. "How could this happen? Is this what Einstein meant when he said time was relative?" I said aloud to my dog Clio, "For crying out loud, Clio, just a second ago I was sixteen and celebrating having a driver's license."

During that celebration, I was dreaming of owning a Harley-Davidson motorcycle. In a moment, I would begin to fantasize about a beautiful young passenger pressing her perky teenage breasts into my back as she sat behind me, her arms wrapped tightly around my waist. I was in teenage heaven.

Clio is a golden retriever. She is a fabulous listener. I love it when she wags her tail. When she is happy, her whole rear section moves left to right—with or without a very expressive wagging tail.

"You OK, Dad?" I asked. I was standing next to his car.

He was sitting in his car, in the driveway. It was any fall night in the late fifties. No more heavy summer humidity in the air. The Connecticut night air was cool now. Bright colorful leaves were starting to fall from trees. He was coming home from work. He had pulled into our driveway at least fifteen minutes ago. Now, as he often did, he turned off the car but kept the radio on so he could listen. His window was down, and his arm was resting on the driver's-side door. If you wanted the window to go up or down, you had to crank it yourself. There was a lever that operated the window; you cranked it inside the car. No push-button electric windows yet. I was nine years old—maybe ten.

"I'm fine, son," he said. "…just listening to the Sox."

He meant the Boston Red Sox. The Boston Red Sox was his baseball team. Mine too.

"It might be on TV, Dad. Would you like me to see if it's on?"

"No, son, this is just fine," he said. "He's *due,* you know."

He meant Ted Williams; he was due to hit a home run. Ted Williams was up at bat. If he had not hit a home run in several games, my dad would always say, "He's due." He was right a lot.

Even in the early sixties, my dad often preferred the radio to the TV, especially for baseball games. Inside the house, he might sit in the living room after he came home from work and had a bite to eat. Usually, at night, his bite to eat was borsht (cold Russian beet soup). He would add a little sour cream. Then he would go into the living room and turn the radio on. Sometimes he would read a newspaper and listen to the voice of Curt Gowdy, the current voice of Boston Red Sox baseball.

When I was a boy, anyone who was sixty-two was old—really old, practically dead. Now it is not so old. Everyone says so. Even my adult children say that. During my twenties, as I reflected on the way I was living, I pretty much thought I'd be dead long before I was sixty-two years old. I was already living far beyond instant gratification; I and many of my peers were working on something called "constant gratification." It was the sixties, you know.

Actually, back in 1969, when I looked around at people who had made it to their sixties and seventies, I thought, "Who in the hell would want to live that long?" or "Who would want to live like that?" What could you do at sixty-something years old besides eat supper at 5:00 p.m., make monthly contributions to the pharmaceutical and medical industries, grow hair in places you never thought possible, and send young men off to war to die in swamps or deserts for reasons never fully explained—or explained in a way that even fourth graders could see through? And sex? Good grief. If there was any, what would sex be like?

On September 28, 1960, Ted Williams ended his baseball career. At his last at bat, he took a swing like he was going for the fences. He missed.

"Jack Fisher into his windup, here's the pitch," said Curt Gowdy over WHDH radio in Boston. "Williams swings, and there's a long drive to deep right. It could be…it *could* be? IT IS! A home run for Ted Williams!"

In 1960, Ted Williams was the eighteenth professional baseball player to end his career this way. I was eleven years old. My dad was fifty-six years old. Ted Williams was forty-two; Curt Gowdy was forty-one; and baseball, as we knew it, was somewhere around one hundred.

The Long-Water-Land People

So I LIVE IN CONNECTICUT. Right here in Wallingford, Connecticut. I was born just down the road in New Haven. I was born here, all right, but I am hardly what you would call a Connecticut Yankee. My family and I are over 220 years too late to America for that distinction.

New Haven, Connecticut, was founded in 1630. Wallingford was founded in 1670, by a group of people from New Haven. My dad was founded in 1904; my mom in 1918. I made my appearance in 1949. I am no Connecticut Yankee, but like Wallingford's founding fathers, I came from New Haven too—a New Haven hospital.

Wallingford is 151 feet above sea level, thirteen miles north of New Haven and Long Island Sound. I won't see it, but if this global warming thing continues, Wallingford might be a new beachfront town in about a hundred years, maybe sooner.

George Washington came through here twice, in 1751 and 1789. I know a couple who live in the home where he stayed when he came through in 1789. In that same year, George Washington was elected to the presidency of the brand-new United States of America.

Lyman Hall, a signer of the Declaration of Independence (for Georgia) was born here; so was Moses Y. Beach, the founder—or rather, organizer—of the Associated Press. We have schools named after them. Aaron Jerome was born here in 1764. Don't feel bad if you don't know who he was. No one knows who he was. But everyone knows his great-great-grandson: Winston Churchill. Historians will tell you that Lyman Hall, like Thomas Jefferson, was a great man. They both owned human beings: slaves. So did George Washington. Apparently, greatness is a lot like the weather: it changes.

The famous prep school Choate-Rosemary Hall is here. When I was a boy, it was the Choate School; just boys, no girls. Choate was founded in 1896. Rosemary Hall, the private girls' school, was founded here, too, in 1890. Rosemary Hall temporarily relocated to Greenwich, Connecticut, but in 1971, the two schools merged here in Wallingford.

The playwright Edward Albee went to Choate; so did John F. Kennedy. So did John Dos Passos, Adlai Stevenson II, Glenn Close, Jamie Lee Curtis, Michael Douglas, and tons more famous folks. Get this: when I was a boy, Michael Douglas was at my house. He was swinging from a door jam at the bottom of some steps that led to my sister's room. Unbeknownst to my parents, who were out, my sixteen-year-old sister Sherry was throwing a little get-together one Saturday night in the early sixties, and he showed up. Choate is only a mile away from our house. Many boys came drunk. "What are you doing?" I asked him. "What's it look like I'm doing, pea brain?" Michael Douglas barked back at me. "What a nitwit," I thought to myself. You know, he looked a little like his father, Kirk, the famous movie actor known to me mostly as Spartacus. It was the chin.

In the fifties, Wallingford was a small, sleepy New England town where everyone knew you had a flat tire before you could get it changed and get into town. It is named after Wallingford, England.

In the spring of 1970, many people from Wallingford, England, came here to celebrate our town's three hundredth birthday. Our town had invited them. To imitate the olden days, men in town grew mustaches and/or beards. I already had both, because I grew up in the sixties. At the time, my beard look went great with my cowboy boots, my bell-bottom jeans, my bleached-denim work shirts, my leather vest, and my denim jacket with the colorful Poo Bear drinking out of a bottle of J&B Scotch skillfully embroidered by a sweetheart of mine on the upper part of its slightly torn left sleeve.

"Know what" I said to Jack, my insurance agent. We were sitting at a bar in Wallingford, Connecticut called Main Street USA. It was 1995. We were drinking Heinekens and I was telling him about a book I wanted to write someday. "I still have that denim jacket. It's hanging up in my garage."

Wallingford, England, is probably about six or seven hundred years older than Wallingford, Connecticut.

Right about the same time Wallingford, England was first being inhabited, the "original people" (that's what the peoples we know as the Quinnipiac Indians called themselves) began living around Wallingford, Connecticut. They also called themselves the Long-Water-Land Nation. The name comes from an Algonquin Indian phrase that describes the Quinnipiac River (a river in central Connecticut) at its mouth going into Long Island Sound.

In 1970, I did not see any Quinnipiac Indians celebrating the three hundredth anniversary of Wallingford. If there are any left, I suspect they were not invited. On the other hand, what would there have been for them to celebrate?

For several hundred years after the white people settled it, except for some wars, most people lived and worked and died right here in this community. Nowadays, there are about forty-five thousand people living here. The majority of people work out of town now. They are born out of town. They die out of town, too. That is because we have 911 now, and 911 is what you dial on your phone when someone gets seriously injured or if an older person stops breathing. An ambulance comes right away and carts us off to the hospital. The hospitals are in the next town, just north of here, and in New Haven to the south. The town north of us is called Meriden. Wallingford does not have a hospital. Like Wallingford, Meriden is named after a town in England. Actually, the Meriden here in Connecticut was part of the Wallingford here until 1727.

In the early fifties, when I was a boy, there were about eighteen thousand people here in Wallingford. Wallingford, England, has about sixty-five hundred people living in their community. The last time Wallingford, Connecticut, had sixty-five hundred people living here was around the time my father was born in 1904. His parents were born in Russia, but he was born here in Wallingford. In the late eighteen hundreds, immigrants (including my paternal and maternal grandparents) came here from all over Europe and Russia to begin new lives in America. They came looking for food, for work, for money, or for religious or political freedom. Most of them found it.

I have postcards my father saved of Wallingford, Connecticut, right around the turn of the twentieth century: trolley cars, horse-pulled carriages parked in town, a beautiful Georgian inn right on a shady tree-lined Main Street, cobblestone streets, mansions on Main Street where all the well-to-do Yankees lived. Postcards were the e-mails or tweets of the early nineteen hundreds. If you went anywhere, or even if you just stayed home, everyone sent them. The stamp to mail them cost one penny.

When I was growing up, practically everyone knew or knew of everyone else in town. Now, like a lot of places today, not a lot of folks really know tons of people in the community they live in anymore. Nowadays, their best friends, their divorced parents, or their aunts, uncles, and cousins are often hundreds and even thousands of miles away, living in communities not even imagined in the fifties.

In the fifties, mommies typically stayed home to care for the children while the daddies worked. As a boy, I walked to elementary school with my two older sisters. In 1956, I was seven years old. It was the golden age of childhood here in the United States. Of course, you could never convince a seven-year-old boy with two older sisters that he was living in the golden age of anything.

"Hold my hand, Dicky," said my oldest sister, Donna. We were on Long Hill Road, about to cross Center Street, a busy main road. In those days, the sidewalk was on the other side of Center Street. We were on our way to Simpson School. I was in first grade. She was in sixth grade. I was carrying a royal-blue lunch box with a picture of superman on it. There was a sandwich of Skippy peanut butter and Welch's grape jelly on white Wonder bread in it, together with a package of Hostess cupcakes. On some days I would stay at school for lunch; other days we would walk home.

What made the "golden age" part true was that our activities were not planned, attended, and governed by *adults*. A kid could breathe. You could be *you* in the fifties—no one was wondering if the activity you were participating in would lead to your ultimate success as a senator, a model, a concert pianist, a professional athlete, or a leader of industry. You could fail, swear, or fall down and scrape your knee or cut your finger. The world would not end.

"First you hold your breath for a bit. Then you take a bunch of deep breaths, then hold some, and then blow them out," he said as he explained the game to me. He was taller than me, so I had to look up at him. He lived behind our house down a steep hill. We were in my backyard. His name was James, but we all called him Butch. He was older than me by at least four years. I was nine years old. I was wearing "snap jack" shoes. They had a big flap where the shoelaces would usually be that snapped open or shut. I loved them. Mine were black. Many of us kids thought they were cool.

"Then, when I tell you," Butch said, "you put your hands over your mouth, pretend to blow, and hold your breath for as long as you can."

After I passed out, he and Skipper carried me up to my house and got my mom. They told my mom no one had ever passed out before. Butch explained in detail to her, "You're just supposed to get really dizzy and unable to walk straight." Then he demonstrated.

When my young friends and I played with my sisters, of course my oldest sister Donna thought she was in charge. She always did. She still does. Now she's a CEO of a child welfare agency in New Jersey. She's still helping children. Sometimes we boys would just walk away. That would quiet her down. That would get her goat.

Superman

HERE WAS A MAJOR FEATURE of my childhood education: in the fall of 1956, in the now-demolished Simpson Elementary School, I was instructed to 'duck and cover' just in case the Russians dropped an atom bomb on us. We used to practice getting under our desks. I was seven.

I was sitting next to Peggy, who had blond hair and blond eyelashes. Today she was wearing a Betty Boop skirt. I mean, her skirt had a picture of Betty Boop on it. She had on low-cut white Keds sneakers with pink laces. In the years to come, I would develop a bit of a crush on her. She played eraser tag better than anyone in the class. In case you do not know, eraser tag is played by putting a blackboard eraser on your head and the head of the person you are to try to tag. The two of you are put on opposites sides of the room. A bell goes off. Now, if you are the "tagger," you must tag the other person before the four-minute timer goes off. If the eraser falls off your head while you are being chased or doing the chasing, you lose. If the tagger does tag the "tagee" within the given time, the person who was tagged loses and must sit down. "Go, go!" shouted Paul. Sitting in the back row, he was encouraging Howie to move faster. Peggy was about to tag him, which would mean she would win for the fourth time in a row.

It would be a while before I would fully comprehend an atom bomb. The word "powerful" came to mind—but, of course, not as powerful as Superman. Every seven-year-old knew how to play eraser tag and that Superman was pretty much more powerful than anything or anyone in the whole universe ever (except for Kryptonite).

We were instructed to get under our desks in case a catastrophe occurred, like an atomic bomb dropped somewhere. We practiced it in every grade, for years. I got really good at it; no one was going to make toast out of me! I call this part of my life the "under the desk period." It was marked by persistent bumps on the top of my head I acquired as I ducked to get under my desk at ever increasing speeds.

Our backyards were our playgrounds, our backyards and at certain times of the year, that private golf course across the street. Lassie, Kathy's collie, was always there. We were her kids. This was her neighborhood. We even explained our games and our play to her, just like Timmy did for TV's Lassie. During the 1950s, after Kathy's mom died and her dad moved them several miles away from Long Hill Road, it felt like she was on the other side of the world. She even went to a different school. In the future, her dad would move them to Cheshire, a town due west of Wallingford. A decade would pass before we would see each other again, and Lassie would disappear into my memory.

In 2009, I turned sixty. Being over sixty was practically enough to send me back under my desk. Turning fifty years old had certainly been an eye-opener, but sixty was a catastrophe.

"Karen," I said, one March day in 2009. Karen is my wife. "Do you realize I'll be sixty next month? It's a catastrophe!" I shouted.

"You'll be fine, honey," she said calmly. "Sixty is the new fifty now. If you live long enough, it happens to everyone."

"Yes, of course it happens to everyone," I said. "But not to *me!*"

So I bought myself a new baseball glove that year. The last one I'd bought was in the eighties. By 2009, I needed to replace my twenty-year-old glove. Now, shopping for a new one in 2009, I experienced a thought I'd never had before. It had to do with my sixtieth birthday and my tendency to frugality.

"Dick, the way you keep things forever, this might be the *last* baseball glove you ever buy," I said out loud to myself on the way to Sports Authority. "Ooh, good grief! You're right. I ought to buy a really nice one."

My son, Tom, was seventeen at the time. My daughter, Samantha, was twenty-three. Six months earlier, in the fall of 2008, my mom had died at the age of ninety. I think she was simply exhausted from life and ready for whatever was next. For months prior to her death, my sister Donna and she had a wonderful ritual. They would sing childhood lullabies together each night before her bedtime.

I have a friend who is writing a book about dogs. He has written a lot of books, but never one about dogs. He told me that in the dog world, it has often been said, "You do not get the dog you want, you get the dog you need."

So I wonder: am I living the life I needed, or the one I wanted? And then I think; how come I do not know?

Fishing Papers

I AM FAMILIAR WITH CATASTROPHE. A long time ago, like young men and women through the ages, I had my heart broken. In my early twenties, I was in love with a beautiful young woman who wanted to marry me. She had a dimple right in the middle of her chin. Actually, she only wanted to marry me sometimes. We dated and lived together, but only for short periods of time. In 1968, we lived in downtown Philadelphia, in a converted-porch apartment so small you'd have to be either lovers or Siamese twins just to survive. In the early seventies, we lived together in Boston on and off. In the winter of 1974, we moved into a house across the street from a very cold, gray Atlantic Ocean in Falmouth, Massachusetts. By then, she was in graduate school at Brandeis. She was very smart—full scholarship and all. She was so smart she'd graduated from an Ivy League college in three years.

In Falmouth, I was working as a carpenter's helper. Early in the mornings, I was writing short stories. Originally I wanted to work on fishing boats, but when I went to apply, a captain told me I needed "fishing papers" to work on a boat.

"So how do I get these fishing papers?"

"Ayaah, I think you have to work on a fishin' boat," said the captain with a straight face and a mischievous Maine accent. "Ayaah, as far as I know, it's the only way to get 'em." It was a regular Joseph Heller moment, if you know what I mean.

So I pounded nails that fall and winter, installing roofs and framing houses. In my spare time, I collected rejection letters from the magazines I sent my short stories to.

I was supposed to be in graduate school, too. Three months after my graduation from Antioch College, in Yellow Springs, Ohio, I was actually in Salt Lake City, Utah. I was preparing to enter the University of Utah to start their MFA program. I was to study to be a writer.

Years earlier, the writer Rod Serling had graduated from Antioch College. Remember *The Twilight Zone*? That was him. He wrote it. He was also to be blamed for all those airline hijackings that started in the late sixties. He wrote a story called "The Doomsday Flight" about a passenger plane that was hijacked in the air and demanded a ransom. To get the ransom, the hijacker rigged the plane so it would blow up if it dropped below four thousand feet. Only he could stop it. Soon after he wrote that story, someone really did hijack a plane. The first *real* hijacker wanted money, lots of money, and he got it. He ordered the plane to land, and he collected his ransom. Then the plane took off again, and somewhere over the Rocky Mountains, the hijacker parachuted out. They never caught the guy. Then soon afterward, another one happened—and then another. Poor Rod Serling wished he'd never written that story. He told reporters he wished he'd written a story about a stagecoach driver, starring the actor John Wayne.

Rod died at the age of fifty, in 1975. John Wayne was sixty-eight years old at the time, and I had just turned twenty-six. In Egypt, Mohamed Atta was seven years old. He didn't know it, but in twenty-six years, he and eighteen of his peers, mostly from Saudi Arabia, would be enlisted to hijack four American passenger planes that they would use to commit religious homicide and suicide by flying them into the World Trade Towers in New York City and the Pentagon in Virginia. One other plane, supposedly destined for the White House, would crash into the countryside of Pennsylvania as brave passengers attempted to retake control. All would die in the attempt.

These events would shock us all, like we were shocked to discover the massive ovens of Auschwitz or Treblinka, where millions of Jews were gassed to death and then burned. When the World Trade Center in New York City came down on September 11, 2001, I was fifty-two years old. I didn't know it at the time, but I would spend the rest of my middle age watching what seemed like a continuous series of ugly, tragic, pathetic doomsday events performed on behalf of god or religion, on behalf of a country or corporation or honor or oil, or even on behalf of something called "quarterly earnings." Apparently, these ghastly events at the beginning of the twenty-first century were intended to bring men and women of strong conviction a variety of rewards to be dished out before and after death: sometimes a one-way ticket to heaven or hundreds of virgins to sleep with; sometimes a windfall of money, a medal for your chest, or the approval of a god or millions in Wall Street profits. For a few, the reward was power: success in running in and winning an election. Winners and losers: Homo sapiens just cannot get enough of this.

George W. Bush was fifty-five years old in 2001. Osama bin Laden was forty-one. Ted Williams was now eighty-two years old. In one year, when Ted Williams died, his children would argue bitterly whether to bury him or to freeze him. Eventually they agreed to have him frozen cryogenically. Here was the plan: upon each of their own deaths, his children all planned to be frozen cryogenically as well. Once the technology was available, they could all be safely unfrozen and be rejoined as a family.

And you thought your family was peculiar?

You won't believe it, but in 1972, right after I graduated from college and moved to Salt Lake City to attend graduate school, I landed a job working in a supermarket. Supermarkets were to take on an unusual role in my life. You'll see.

This owner of this Salt Lake City supermarket bought many cases of goods containing broken items from the large distribution centers in the area; he might purchase a case of twelve bottles of ketchup, for example, one of which was broken. He got these cases at incredibly discounted prices. It was my job to stand over a big tub sink, put on thick, waterproof gloves, wash the other eleven bottles, dry them, price them, and put them on the shelves. I also drove the truck that picked up these fantastic buys.

The man who owned the supermarket had a very pretty daughter, who had a crush on me. At twenty-three years of age, I mustered up all my available good sense and stayed clear of her. At the time, she was a senior in high school. She used to come by the slop sink several times a week, exploring thoughts and feelings I thought she would do better to pursue in the future, with someone younger than me.

Salt Lake City was a funny place. I wasn't sure why, but I was sure I was miserable. I was lonely. I needed an excuse to leave, and school wouldn't even begin for another month. My mom had sent me a care package. I picked it up at the post office and then went to do my laundry. When I came out, I discovered someone had broken into my car and stolen the package.

I was on the road back to Boston the next day. Even the cloudless blue skies overhead could not convince me to stay. No graduate school for me. I would work and write real stories and drink in real bars with real men, shoot some pool, and get my stories published for real cash money.

I have hidden it well, but I have always been a restless soul. In the old days, I was a card-carrying "the grass is greener" kind of guy. I was committed to joy, happiness, and ease. There may have been a speck of immaturity in my character—well, perhaps a little more than a speck.

Like most earthlings, unbeknown to me, I was on a collision course with events that would sadden and shock me, altering my notions of the how and the where of my life I would live on this planet. For about a second, once I graduated from college, I would think I was finally all grown up. For that same second, I would feel like I'd have all the time in the world to make decisions—what to do, when to do it, and where. I could fail or find success or maybe just get "walked" to first base. But circumstance would catch up with me, unfold its arms and invite me in, and insist that I participate here on earth in a certain way. Unbeknownst to me, by the early fall of 1973, someone in the know might have said to me, "Hey, chief, time as you know it is very short." In a moment, someone else could have added, "The old clock is ticking, Dicky-boy."

One night in 1974, the teenage son of the mayor of Falmouth, Massachusetts, smashed right into my parked yellow 1967 Olds Cutlass on Surf Drive. The yellow Oldsmobile was a convertible with bucket seats. He totaled my parked car, but miraculously neither he nor his girlfriend was hurt much. The very smart, pretty girl with the dimple on her chin who would never marry me when I asked her to but often wanted to marry me when I did not and I brought him and his girlfriend inside our house, sat them down on our sofa, and then called the police—there was no 911 then, and no one sounded like or looked like they were in need of a doctor or a hospital. The teenage driver smelled like a can of Budweiser.

In Falmouth, as on the rest of Cape Cod, "the season" was late springtime through early fall—the college and public school vacation months. If you wanted to rent this cottage during those months, even in the seventies, you would have to drive there with a carload of gold bars for the landlord just to stay for a week or two. We rented in the *off-season*: late fall, winter, and early spring. In the off-season, pretty graduate students and their roofer boyfriends could afford to rent houses on the Cape, even if they were right across the street from the cold, gray Atlantic Ocean.

Here is what we did for years. We would live together and then break up. Then some time would pass, and we would get back together, only to eventually break up again. Once in a while, this lovely woman with the long brown hair, and sometimes bangs, would collect herself or get so angry at me she would no longer want to marry me. As soon as this moment occurred, I would of course ask her to marry me. She would be too angry with me to consider marriage. Her anger might have had something to do with our breakups; most of the time, I would tell her I was leaving her. Why would I leave her? No one knew. Not even me. What was I going to tell her, that I was a restless soul?

I even brought a ring with me once while asking her to marry me. She had recently decided not to have anything to do with me. The ring was my mother's. I drove it down to Philadelphia, where she was attending the University of Pennsylvania. I proposed. She, of course, said no. I went back to college, miserable and inconsolable—until next time.

"Are you all right?" I said to the driver that night. I said it loudly, because the tide was coming in and the Atlantic Ocean surf was up. The breaking waves were only about one hundred yards from the road.

"I think I'm OK," the mayor's son said. "Check on my girlfriend."

It was dark. I hadn't noticed anyone else in the car, but there she was. She looked helpless; her long blond hair hid her pretty face, and she seemed lost, dazed, and confused. She was bent over, leaning forward in the front seat. I went around to the passenger side and opened the door. She was waking up.

"Are you OK?" I asked again.

"I think so," she said. "What happened?" There was some blood on her forehead, but I could not really see. Her door was open, but there was no overhead light on in the car anymore.

"Your car hit my parked car," I said. "What's your name?"

"Cindy," Cindy said. "I want to get out."

"Let me help you, Cindy." I held out my arm. "Grab my arm."

Neither car looked very good. Those two were very lucky on that night—everyone but the cars survived.

When the police arrived, no matter what I told them, the only thing they wanted to know was how fast I was driving my parked car.

The Starting Line

My mother was a stunning beauty from New Haven, Connecticut. She was a real head-turner, everyone said so. Her name was Evelyn. She was born in the fall of 1918, just one month from the end of World War 1. When she was born, being a woman, she and millions of other women did not have the right to vote here in the United States. That would change before she was two years old.

She was pretty. She was so pretty that when she was a senior in high school during the late thirties, several of her teachers asked her out on dates. In those days, you could do that without risking arrest for child abuse. Sometimes she dated young men at Yale University on their ways to becoming fabulously wealthy doctors, lawyers, politicians, bankers, and big-shot owners of baseball and basketball teams. Her own family had lost all its money in the 1929 stock market crash, eleven years after she was born. In the twenties, before the crash, they were rich—very rich.

Morris Puklin, my mom's grandfather, arrived on Ellis Island in the early 1890s. He came from Moscow. He was sixteen years old. He was bright, he was educated, and he looked older than he was. He would look that way for the rest of his life. He spoke and wrote two languages, Russian and Yiddish. He went directly to New Haven and secured a full-time job paying a booming six dollars per week.

Soon he learned a third language in night school: English. He saved enough in three years to be able to open a business, a retail cigar company. He did well, and years later he sold that company and began a wholesale stationery and merchandise business. He was so successful that within ten years he needed six salesmen and eight warehouse workers to process the $300,000 worth of business the company was doing each year before 1914. Eventually, he would bring his oldest son, Herbert (my mother's father) into the business. Herbert was the treasurer. Life was good when the war ended. My mother remembers a chauffeur driving her and her mother around New Haven when she was a little girl.

In 1929, however, what my mother's family did not lose in the stock market, they lost in the banks. In the twenties, they were rich. In the thirties, they were dirt poor. It goes like that sometimes. After high school, my mother worked in dress shops as a salesgirl. Her father, Herbert, became a postman. Life went on, and the Depression settled in. Morris, now in his sixties, did not have the energy for, or simply could not find his way back to the magic of that American dream he had created twice before in years gone by.

After they lost all their money, the family lived in a two-family house at 229 Norton Street, in New Haven, Connecticut. It was one block away from Whalley Avenue. Two famous Jewish delicatessens were situated across the street from each other down on that corner: Al's and Chuck's. Al and Chuck knew each other. Those delis are all gone now. So are Al and Chuck. So are all the Jews from this neighborhood. The fortunate ones moved out to Westville or Woodbridge, the fancy suburbs of New Haven, and then retired down to Florida to play cards, golf, swim, and drive health-care and restaurant workers to look for new careers in other parts of the country.

"He was a prince…I'm telling you, a prince," Mrs. Rabinowitz told the Miami, Florida ER physician with tears in her eyes. The doctor had the unfortunate task of informing her of the death of Irving Rabinowitz, her husband of forty-one years. Irving, who'd had a heart attack less than fifty minutes earlier, was seventy-five years old. Rachel Rabinowitz was seventy-two. They had been retired living in Florida for the past seven years. In 1947, after the war, they had left Germany for America to start over. A Jewish man in Newark, New Jersey, sponsored them. The Jewish man in New Jersey did not know them. All he knew was they were survivors. They both had survived the Buchenwald concentration camp. They had settled in Brooklyn near other survivors.

The doctor knew Mr. Rabinowitz was a survivor from the camps. He did not need to ask. He saw the numbers branded on Mr. Rabinowitz forearm. When Jews and others arrived at these camps, they were *registered*. They were branded on their forearms like they were cattle.

After high school, Evelyn worked in dress shops, but not for long.

Evelyn dated those college boys, but she did not fall for them. She fell for a high school graduate. He had no college. She fell for a hard-working grocer named Tommy, from Wallingford, Connecticut. He was no kid. She was twenty years young. He was already thirty-four: a grown man. He was handsome. He was nice. Everyone called him Tom or Tommy. Practically everyone liked him. Those college students did not have a chance. He owned his business. He was a grocer. He also owned land and buildings.

She lived on Norton Street. Sometimes he sent a car to 229 Norton Street to pick her up. Did I tell you he was nice, and everyone really liked him? They dated in 1939. They married in 1940. As his only son, I can tell you this with certainty: in Wallingford, Connecticut, or anywhere else in the world, he was one very tough act to follow.

22

Like many people, Evelyn's folks on Norton Street had a lot of worries during the Depression. But they did not have to worry about food anymore. Tom sent food to them from his grocery store every week.

Tom's own father had also come to America from Russia in the 1890s. His father's name was Samuel. Samuel was a young man from a small Russian city in the middle of nowhere where Jewish people were occasionally slaughtered for "blood libel." The name of the city was Vilna. Blood libel was based on the myth that Jewish families killed Christian children to drink their blood during certain Jewish holidays. Every time a little child died, Jewish people were butchered. Samuel and thousands of others came to America partially because, in the 1890s, the Cossacks had been doing some ethnic cleansing. But mostly they came because there was nothing in Russia for them, certainly nothing that even remotely resembled a future.

Samuel's family farmed the land. They lived outside this city. Samuel listed himself as a butcher, but his true love was for horses: caring for them, riding them, trading them.

After arriving, within three years he sent word back to his family that he had need of a wife. The family back in Russia hired a matchmaker (I'm not making this up!) who made the match, and one Dora Harrison was sent from Vilna to marry the farmer, butcher, and horseman Samuel Caplan of Wallingford, Connecticut.

Dora Harrison was the daughter of educated Jewish merchants, townspeople who could read and write and add and subtract. The only things Samuel could read were animal tracks in the dirt or snow, weather patterns in the sky, and the size and quality of a future horse by its appearance as a foal. Samuel did not know Dora before she came to America. Dora had never seen Samuel. Can you believe this?

"Imagine, a matchmaker," I told my friend Ben at Antioch College in 1969. "Can you dig it?" I was twenty years old, in college, and ready for most anything. My lottery number was 191. I will get to that later. Seventy-five years earlier, my paternal grandfather was working eight thousand miles away in the fields just outside Vilna, Russia, and dreaming of America. He, like his brothers, tilted his head to the side and kept one eye out on the horizon for Cossacks on horses, galloping across the plains.

In the late 1890s, once married and settled, Dora enacted the Russian Harrison Family Plan explained to her by her father: one by one, year by year, she sent for (sponsored) a brother to come to America—now they had an address to come to, an occupation, and the promise of a job. They were all to be butchers in the Caplan family meat market. I am not sure, but I don't think any of them ever worked a day in that little hole-in-the-wall store.

But in the years to come, Dora and her second-born son, when he was old enough, ran the little store. She and her second-born son grew the business. Her baby son was too young. Her oldest had no interest. Her husband traded horses, bought horses, rode horses, fed horses, sold horses, took care of horses, admired horses. She spoke little English. She taught her second son the principles of retail: buying, selling, being fair and honest, always saving most of the profits, and then reinvesting them in your own business. He was her English ears. He was her strong back. He was a natural. After he graduated high school, she was his college courses; she was his MBA, too.

Tom's parents were a little like the Puritans from England. They came to America for religious freedom. Equally important, they also came to avoid what most believed to be a life of certain poverty, inequality, and misery.

The Building

THE LARGEST COMMERCIAL BUILDING IN downtown Wallingford was located right on North Main Street, 25–45 North Main Street, to be exact. One hundred feet long, fifty feet wide, and over seventy feet high, it had two-and-a-half-foot-thick stone foundations, wooden beams so big you would think it'd be stronger than kryptonite, and walls three bricks thick. Fancy Portland, Connecticut, brownstone was used on the front ground floor to show off the look of it. Open the interior walls on the third floor, and you would find beams so big you would have thought they came from sequoia trees. High above, going across the front of the roof, was a white picket fence. Although it was removed many years ago, the center of the roof once held a gigantic cupola. "*The Building*" had twenty thousand square feet to lease and another five thousand feet of usable space in the basement. It was over a half a block long. It may not have been very impressive by today's big-city standards, but in a small New England town, in the fifties, it was still thought to be grand.

Construction began in 1857. It would take nearly seven years to complete because of the Civil War. William, one of the Wallace brothers from Prospect, Connecticut, was building it. When I said he built it, I mean he designed it, purchased all the materials, and managed its construction. He was a remarkable man. The original idea was for stores to be at ground level, with offices and a hotel on the upper floors. Mr. Wallace planned to open a grocery store in the building. The first sidewalks in Wallingford were built in front of the building, because he fought for them. The building's official name in those days was the Professional Building, because it housed practically every kind of profession practiced in small-town America at the turn of the century. The Good Templars hired the hall on the top floor in 1869. On the second floor, it housed the Wallingford Library Association (established April 1, 1883), then called the Ladies' Library Reading Room. In 1892, the Crescent Social Club rented space; the Ramblers Bicycle Club in 1893; the Veteran Firemen's Association in 1893, and the Eureka Club in 1897.

From the mid-1860s to the 1960s, on sidewalk level, the building housed druggists, grocers, clothing stores, jewelers, confectioners, tailors, tin merchants, meat markets, saloons, barbers, boot and shoe stores, plumbers, law offices, hairdressers, bakers, millinery, insurance companies, paper hangers, and restaurants.

My dad thought this building would be a great location for their growing grocery and meat store. During the Roaring Twenties, Caplan's Market had found success and already had relocated once to larger quarters on the main commercial street in Wallingford, Center Street. Business boomed during the twenties. But now, in 1931, the biggest building in Wallingford was up for sale because America had hit a large bump in the road of capitalism in 1929. The unregulated stock market had fallen so far, so fast most people did not even have time to be terrified. One day they had a buck; the next they had *bupkis*—the Yiddish word for nothing, nada, zip, zero. Buildings all over America were up for sale because Newton's laws of gravity were stronger than Adam Smith's laws of capitalism. Industrial capitalism was in need of a major tune-up. No one was shopping; no one was paying any bills; no one was spending much of anything except for the necessities: bread, beer, cigarettes, and hard liquor.

The president of the Wallingford Bank & Trust, which now owned the building on North Main Street, was not fond of Jewish people.

"What are you doing here?" he said to the twenty-seven-year-old Tom Caplan. His tone was nasty. His face reflected impatience, arrogance, and disgust. Tom Caplan handed him his bid to buy the building. The banker looked at the bid and laughed. It was a mean laugh, punctuated with sarcasm and delivered with righteous anger. The banker's attitude was nothing new for the handsome Jew. As a boy and a teenager, like many children of immigrants, he had experienced his share of unwelcoming comments from Yankees, both the young ones and ones who had lived here for generations. They maintained—or rather commanded—status and seniority thanks to the history of their forebears. He wasn't sure if the anger had more to do with his religion or his immigrant parents. His bid for the building was $25,000.

"You will never own this building," the Yankee banker barked at Tom Caplan. Then he invited the young man to leave. Later that day, someone would offer $26,000. Tom Caplan raised his bid again, and so did this unknown bidder. It went on like that for a couple of days.

Late that Friday afternoon, Tom Caplan dropped off his third bid for the property. This one was for $29,500. After submitting the bid, he went straight to his favorite speakeasy to have a scotch and soda. Tom's father drank vodka—Russian vodka, when possible. Like so many Americans, Tom drank scotch. He was assimilating. There were so many speakeasies in Wallingford that no one minded prohibition anymore.

A man sitting at the bar was complaining that every time he put in a bid to buy the building at 25–45 North Main Street, someone would out bid him by $1,000. Tom Caplan was seated next to the complaining man. In fact, the complaining man was a good friend of the nice Tom Caplan. Tom Caplan asked his friend for a favor. The man snickered. Then he wholeheartedly agreed.

Weeks later, the president of the Wallingford Bank & Trust Company scheduled the closing of the sale of the property in question. It was three in the afternoon of September 30, 1931. The attorney for the bank was there. The papers were ready. Tom Caplan walked in with his attorney and the friend who had put the bid in for him. The bank president asked Tom Caplan's friend what the Jew was doing there. The friend told him he had just bought the building and was here to close the deal: the last bid he'd handed him was for his friend Tom Caplan, not himself. After Tom Caplan signed the papers, the banker never spoke to either one of them again.

Other people who knew the banker would think that a blessing.

A Piece of Fruit

In 1948, Evelyn Caplan was turning thirty years old, and she was all done having babies. She had been married to Tom for almost nine years, and it wasn't like she hadn't had babies. She had delivered three times, all girls. The first baby had died within days of birth. "Baby girl" is what it says on the little stone monument in the Jewish cemetery on the road over the bridge that goes nowhere on the other side of the railroad tracks near the big factory that makes plastics and cancer.

This loss was followed by the births of two healthy baby girls right after World War II ended. In 1948, the girls were one and three years old. Now she was letting anyone who would listen know that she was all done ruining her figure with pregnancies. At the monthly Hadassah meeting at Beth Israel Synagogue, she told her good friend Edith, "No more babies for me. I'm all done looking like a piece of ripe fruit." But my father, then forty-four years of age, lobbied for one more. In 1948, some people in town said he had it all. Well, almost all: a gorgeous wife whom he loved and who loved him, two sweet daughters, his own home, friends, money, land, a successful business. He had it all, but he wanted a son.

I was born in April of 1949. Like my two sisters, I took my place in the post-World War II generation beginning in the mid-forties and going right on into the early sixties.

"Right on" is something my generation said often. We said it during the sixties, when the oldest among us were teenagers, graduating high school on our way to attend college. It was meant to confirm with enthusiasm what someone else had just said. It was our version of what our parents had said when they were young and good or interesting news showed up in their lives—a rare commodity during a depression and a world war. "Swell!" they said.

We said "Far out!" Our parents would never say, "Far out." It meant "that's amazing!" or more confirmation with enthusiasm. We were big on explanation by extreme overstatement. Something wasn't just a certain way in 1968; it was the most certain way that a thing could ever be. Our everyday speech lived in the superlative. We also said "Can you dig it?" or "I can dig it," meaning can you enjoy it, or can you believe or understand it? As a statement, it was the frosting on the cake, the proper response to "Far out!"

"Far out!" cried the pretty girl in the miniskirt. She had on a T-shirt and was clearly not wearing a bra. Her breasts were declaring freedom from oppressive underclothing. Many young women no longer wore bras. You could tell she was not wearing a bra because her nipples poked out from inside her T-shirt and stood there for everyone not to look at, and when she skipped, her breasts moved with the freedom of a golden retriever off the leash.

"I can dig it," said the young man with the mustache in the bell-bottom jeans. He wore no shoes, and his feet were filthy. No one cared.

Had I been born a decade earlier, I'd have said, "Cool, man!" We used the word "cool," but we were just imitating the older kids. Our replacement for this late fifties adjective was "groovy" or "funky." The older kids, the generation before us, was the "beat generation"—Beatniks.

They said "man" a lot. They said, "Daddy-O," and we said, "Dude." You remember these beats: the writer Jack Kerouac, the poet Allan Ginsberg, the time-traveler Neal Cassady, the poet Gary Snyder and the Merry Pranksters, San Francisco's poet Lawrence Ferlinghetti and his famous bookstore City Lights...They were the generation that came into their early adulthood during the late forties and fifties. They loved modern jazz. The young men had goatees and wore berets; the women wore black leotards. Young people played bongos and attended poetry readings. Everyone smoked cigarettes. They were the initial out-of-the-mainstream youth culture. In the sixties, the beatniks would evolve into the hippies, the counterculture generation. Jack Kerouac would be replaced by Ken Kesey or Kurt Vonnegut, Jr. or Joseph Heller. I read them all.

In the sixties, Dylan's raspy voice and challenging lyrics exploded onto the music scene. Rock and roll music was taking on a life of its own. It too was evolving. It was loud, it was soft; it was provocative, it was traditional. It was drugs, it was death, it was news, it was money; it was more money...

Sha Na Na, a fifties revival rock and roll band from New York City, formed in the late sixties. At the Woodstock Music Festival, they played from 7:30 a.m. till 8:00 a.m. on Sunday, August 18, 1969, right before Jimi Hendrix closed the three-day event.

At Woodstock, Jimi Hendrix was twenty-seven years old. Richard Nixon was fifty-six. I was twenty, and Barack Obama had just turned eight. My mom was fifty-two years old, and Elvis Presley was forty-two. Seven years before the Woodstock Music Festival, at the age of thirty-six, Marilyn Monroe had died.

Max Yasgur's Farm

IN THE SIXTIES, BLACK MUSIC evolved—or, rather, erupted—into new descriptive adjectives and adverbs: "soulful," "funky," "outta sight." There was the Detroit sound: the Jackson Five, the Temptations, the Supremes, Aretha Franklin, the Four Tops, Martha and the Vandellas, Smokey Robinson and the Miracles. There was Otis Redding and James Brown from the South, and a lot of music that was harder to categorize—Ray Charles, or Roberta Flack, or Dionne Warwick. Young white high school and college kids began to purchase this music so fast that new stores selling records were popping up all over the place. In the fifties, young people bought records called forty-fives: they had one song on each side and a big hole in the middle of the record to enter it on the flat spinning table of the record player. In the sixties, something called record albums, with six to eight songs on each side of a much larger vinyl record, made their debut.

The sound of white music was more regional. The New York sound included Simon and Garfunkel, the Lovin' Spoonful, and Carole King. The English sound included the Beatles, the Rolling Stones, the Moody Blues, Jethro Tull, the Animals, Fleetwood Mac, Cream, Cat Stevens, and Donovan. From New England, we had people like Arlo Guthrie and Jonathan Edwards. Then there was the Southern sound of the Marshall Tucker Band and the Allman Brothers. Of course there was the wild West Coast music of the

Jefferson Airplane, the Grateful Dead, Credence Clearwater Revival, Linda Ronstadt, Jackson Brown, The Eagles, the Jimmy Hendrix Experience, the Byrds, Sly and the Family Stone, and the Beach Boys. Texas gave us Janis Joplin, and from New Orleans, Dr. John. Detroit gave us Mitch Ryder and the Detroit Wheels; Chicago produced the Paul Butterfield Blues Band; from Canada came the Band and Leonard Cohen; and from Minnesota we got the one and only Robert Zimmerman—a.k.a. Bob Dylan.

By the mid-sixties, there was nothing beat about us. The beat generation of the early fifties was somewhat apolitical. There was nothing apolitical about us. The poets of the beat generation and several very brave black people had engaged in protests, but many others never uttered a word in protest or congregated to rally against this or that. By the sixties, boomers were exploding into the evening news by demonstrating on college campuses, marching on Washington, DC, rallying to end the Vietnam War, going to the South to march and fight for civil rights, women marching and demanding equal pay, attending music festivals outside where hundreds of thousands of us gathered, and so on and so on.

There was nothing beat about us until years later, in 2008, when the economy collapsed so completely you would have thought there was another depression. In fact, in 2009, 2010, 2011, 2012, 2013, and 2014 everyone *did* think it was a depression. Everyone, that is, except the experts. Millions of people were losing their jobs, companies were going broke, stores were going out of business, and thousands of people in every state lost their homes. Thousands of young people graduated from colleges and graduate schools during those years so they could go work part-time and say, "Would you like fries with that burger?" or "Welcome to Walmart." By 2011, Europe looked so beaten up you'd have thought they were on the wrong end of a Mexican drug deal gone badly. People were wondering if whole countries in Europe were going to go belly-up. But this is a conversation for down the road.

In the sixties, we were still an unnamed generation. Soon we would be the hippies, the love generation. We would be the counterculture. We would electrify most of those beat folk guitars of the fifties. On July 25, 1965, Bob Dylan would play at the annual Newport Folk Festival again as he had for the past two years. He would shock them all that day by playing some electric guitar with a group called the Paul Butterfield Blues Band. The times were changing, all right. Soon someone would have to reinvent record players, speakers, and amplifiers. Then we would invent 8-track sound machines, then tape machines, then discs and disc players until finally, in the twenty-first century, record buying and radio listening gave way to downloading a music disc or a computer address called Pandora or iTunes.

And we would shock the world when a small gathering of us, about a half a million or so, got together for a casual weekend to listen to some music outdoors on Max Yasgur's dairy farm in the hills of New York State in August 1969. I did not go. While a half a million young people got together to party on Mr. Yasgur's farm in Woodstock, I had to work in my dad's supermarket stocking shelves, sweeping floors, and making hamburger—lots of hamburger. As I will soon explain, I did not *have* to work, but I *had* to work.

In the sixties, there was a girl living in Wallingford, and having a difficult go of it. Eventually she would write an autobiographical book covering her late adolescence and early adulthood called *Riding in Cars with Boys*. The girl's name was Beverly Donofrio. The book was very successful. In 2001, the TV and movie actress Penny Marshall made a film out of it. Drew Barrymore played Beverly. Beverly's father was a policeman in town. It was fairly well known among young men in Wallingford that it was a good idea to avoid the company of this particular cop.

Beverly was hardly a hippie. But she did take the nontraditional route to higher education; she became a single mother very early in life. She was rolling the dice and looking for a six the hard way.

During the early sixties, she thought over and over, "I will become a writer." It only took her some sixteen more years after high school. In 1986, she completed her master's. In 1990, she published *Riding in Cars with Boys*. She was forty years old. I was forty-one.

If you talk to the right people, they will tell you not to give up on attaining the things you really want in life. Some people talk about talent. My friend Ben says, "Never mind about talent. Just stick with stamina. Stick with stamina and be consistent. Write. If you want to be a writer, write every day."

Heartbreak Planet

I THINK I HAD ALREADY fallen in love with parades before I could walk. It was the drums that did it—the beat. It was the syncopation; it was the rhythm; it was the marching. In middle school, I took up the snare drum so I could march in a parade one day. It was people dressed in uniform in the middle of the road. It was the horses, the old cars, the fife and drum corps, the marching high school bands, and of course it was the toys the venders sold that you only see at parades. But most of all, I waited for the soldiers. As a boy growing up in the fifties, Wallingford's Memorial Day Parade was everything a boy could ever want out of a parade. It had everything.

The World War I veterans rode in the backseats of spotless, just-washed convertibles. Sometimes their wives sat right beside them. Most wore civilian clothes. The World War II veterans were dressed in their military uniforms from the forties. So were the Korean War veterans from the early fifties. They marched neatly in rank and file; someone always called the cadence. Often there were enough of them that all the services were represented, and they marched separately: army, navy, air force, and marines. My eyes would widen as they passed. They all had guns: rifles tilted over their shoulders. The officers had side-arms. Some wore white gloves. Some rode on jeeps. Some carried flags. Many had medals on their uniforms.

Many of my friends' fathers had gone to war in Europe and the South Pacific during the forties. Some of them marched in this very parade. Many of their grandfathers had gone to war in that same Europe back in 1917–1918.

In 1913, my nine-year-old father watched men who fought in America's Civil War march down North Main Street. This very parade, Memorial Day, was started in the mid-1860s to honor the fallen soldiers of that war. Later on in the twentieth century, they would include soldiers who died in all of America's wars. During my dad, Tom Caplan's lifetime, he would watch veterans from the Civil War, the Spanish-American War, World War I, World War II, the Korean War, and the Vietnam War march down North Main Street.

My own father, born in 1904, was too young for World War I, and he was rejected for service in World War II due to bad knees. Missing out on going to war—that did not happen too often. History books sometimes report a break in the action, a kind of golden age of life on the planet when love and respect for our fellow man was demonstrated everywhere. Don't believe it. There have always been so many wars and so much slaughter on the planet that a better name for earthlings might be: *beings of incorrigible behavior and armed conflict*, and a better name for earth: *Heartbreak Planet*.

Growing up on Long Hill Road, there were just the good guys and the bad guys. We (Americans) were the good guys. The Communists (the Russians) were the bad guys. I cannot speak with clarity about these good and bad guys anymore; I think I have lived too long. While I do not fully understand all the complications of good and bad now, I do get the enormous complexity of it all, and the dreadful consequences when we attempt to simplify it. But on Long Hill Road, for most of the fifties, it was pretty clear *we* were the good guys. Years would go by before I could imagine us not being the good guys. Years would go by, all right, and then by the mid-sixties, many of us would revisit this good-guy–bad-guy business. We would wonder if Roy Rogers and Dale Evans, or Paladin from the TV show *Have Gun—Will Travel,* or the Lone Ranger or Tonto could right the wrongs in our communities anymore. We would begin to wonder if Perry Mason could deliver justice anymore—especially in Selma, Alabama, or Jackson, Mississippi.

Wallingford's police marched in the parade, too. By the mid-sixties, some of us were questioning the police as part of the good-guy group, someone to call for help, someone to admire, someone to trust. *Dragnet's* stars Jack ("Just the facts, ma'am") Webb and Harry Morgan seem to have disappeared from the landscape.

In the seventies, at that Memorial Day parade I fell in love with, I would watch the ragtag veterans of the Vietnam conflict *walk* right down North Main Street after the veterans of the Korean War. These new Vietnam veterans did not march, nor did they all wear the neat uniforms they were once issued. In my town, they walked casually. Many wore the outfits one could imagine they wore in the jungles of Southeast Asia. Some had torn pants; some of them had rolled up their GI-issued shirt sleeves. Some had apparently rubbed dirt on their faces, as they might have done in the jungle to hide themselves or protect themselves from the bugs. Some did not wear helmets; they wore bandanas on their heads like pirates. They were not neat, but they certainly walked with honor. They did not smile. They did not wave at the viewers who clapped or at the children who waved at them. They carried black-and-white flags that represented the MIAs: the missing in action. They did not look like soldiers; they looked like angry warriors.

There was a veteran from World War II who marched every year and would play taps. Long ago, he had been in the Marine Corps. His name was Al, and he was a good friend of my father's. He was a musician, as well as a soldier. He had a metal plate in his head from a wound he had suffered during the war. The parade would stop at a certain place, and he would play taps. Blocks away and hidden, when his daughter was old enough and could play a strong enough trumpet, she played the echo. If the metal plate in his head affected his well-being or his cognition, it certainly did not affect the way he played the trumpet. And his teenage daughter played taps like it was something she had been doing for the past forty years. It was a sacred moment.

I don't know much, but I can assure you of this: in the United States, Memorial Day parades will have a secure future. Across the country, in 1970, taps would need to be played for all those newly killed in the Vietnam War, as well as for all those past wars—and for future wars we did not even know about, as far as the eye could see.

In 1970, Colin Powell was a soldier in Vietnam. He was thirty-three years old. Dick Cheney was twenty-nine. During the Vietnam War, Dick Cheney received five deferments from military service. When asked about these deferments in the eighties, when he served as secretary of defense, he said, "I had other priorities in the sixties than military service."

"Me too," I told Clio, my current sweet golden retriever. Except when she falls asleep, she keeps an eye on me when I am around.

A 10-13

ONE DAY LATE IN THE nineteen sixties, badge number 19076 decided to do the impossible. At the time, of course, he did not know it was impossible. Neither did I. Neither did anyone. He was born in 1936, in the Brooklyn borough of New York City. Saving a police department—all by yourself—that does not want to be saved is not a simple task. Like me, he thought that they, the police, were supposed to be the good guys. Badge number 19076 had noticed that many policemen in the department were misbehaving. So he spoke to his superiors. He spoke to them, but he was, as the poet said, just "blowing in the wind." Those bosses were on the take, too. Eventually, he would be taught a lesson. Some lessons are hard; some are easy. Some people thought this lesson was harder than a petrified forest.

Many thought he was set up. A setup is just like it sounds. In this case, the man's peers made sure he ended up in a bad situation. In this case it was in front of a man with a gun who would shoot him.

But in spite of being shot in the face, he did not die. The event was a drug bust. The New York City policemen who came with him left him on his own. His backup was not there.

All police immediately call a 10-13 when a cop is down. Every cop who hears a 10-13 is expected to respond *immediately*. In this case, no cop at the scene even called an ambulance. But luckily for badge 19076, the guy across the hall from the apartment they were raiding did call.

The policeman now bleeding from his face on the floor of the apartment building in New York City was the youngest son of two Italian immigrants, Vincenzo and Maria Giovanna Serpico. Frank Serpico was a veteran. He'd served in the Korean War.

After he recovered from the gunshot, Frank Serpico, now deaf in one ear, exposed many of his fellow officers and superiors who received graft—payola, bribes—and other illicit gains. These crimes were perpetrated by the white knights, from the street patrol and officers to the big shots running whole divisions in the New York City police department.

"What happened to all the good guys?" some young people said in the late sixties and in the early seventies. "Where did they go?"

"Oh, grow up!" said some older people.

In Dayton, Ohio, in the spring of 1968, the cops just stood there with their shiny helmets on—at least fifty of them, so still. It looked like they were practicing to be a cement wall. Their nightsticks were out, and they were prepared to use them. Gas masks dangled from their belts. They were on their best intimidating behavior. One of them was talking into a bullhorn to the crowd of several hundred young college students holding signs to stop the war in Vietnam.

"You have five minutes to leave the area," the bullhorn said. "If you do not leave the area, we will arrest you and take you to jail."

There they were, in freshly pressed white shirts, blue uniforms, black helmets, and polished black shoes. We, the students, were in worn, torn, faded jeans, tie-dyed T-shirts, sneakers, boots, or sandals. None of our boots were polished. They had guns; we had signs. The signs said STOP THE WAR. We had, according to the police, recently become the enemies of America. There was something happening here, all right. It would be like this for years to come—in Boston, in

Berkeley, in New York, in Chicago, in Miami, in Philadelphia, at colleges and universities all over the country.

"Hey, I got to find a bathroom," I told my friend Ben.

When I came back, he had been arrested in Dayton, Ohio, for behavior unbecoming of a college student in the United States.

A Humanistic Flaw

WE BOOMERS HAD ACCESS TO more education than any generation who came before us. In the United States, more of us than ever before stayed in school forever. People said that to obtain the right job in the sixties or seventies, you needed a college degree. I graduated high school, and like many of us, I just kept going. We studied and then studied some more. For many of us, higher education was a present from parents or grandparents who grew up in the Depression and learned how to save a buck.

We learned about the conflicts in the world, past and present. Human beings were constantly having conflicts with each other— everywhere and forever. Soldiers of one kind or another had been marching for thousands and thousands of years.

We learned that many of these armed conflicts had been staged to compete for natural resources or to eliminate other races/religions/ cultures who might also be attempting to gather those same resources. We learned that human beings in positions of power who had more of everything than they could ever use or need employed human beings who were poor and hungry and had hardly a pot to pee in, to kill off other human beings of a different races, cultures, or religions. While human beings do many things well, that old kindergarten lesson of *sharing* has never been widely utilized once a being was big enough to hold a sword, shoot a gun, throw a rock, fire a slingshot, throw a knife or a fist, shoot an arrow, or chuck a spear.

Many boomers grew up with religion. Many families made their way to religious gatherings on most weekends, or at least on certain holidays. Some of us even attended religious school during the week to learn how to go through certain rites of passage in our early teenage years. I did.

Lots of us do not believe in religion anymore. Others believe in religion so much that they do not believe in much of anything else. One of the features of the late twentieth century and the present day is that considerable numbers of religious people and political talk show radio hosts have decided that it was time for 'reason' to take a back seat to 'opinion'. This opinion had something to do with showing your anger. Leaders of this angry moment are constantly on the TV or the radio or the Internet. They are all very upset. Often these angry leaders are either political candidates or religious leaders.

I remember the following moments from my adolescence and early adulthood. In the 1960s, we killed little girls coming out of Sunday school because their skin was black. We killed young college students who had the audacity to help people vote. We killed more college students for protesting war. We killed a man who was president and another who wanted to be. We killed religious leaders who believed in peaceful protests to achieve basic civil rights. I will tell you about them soon.

This sad moment has been happening on and off for centuries. Sometimes we just killed one or three; sometimes we killed hundreds, or thousands or tens of thousands. We even have names for these moments: one was called the Crusades; another the Inquisition; one was called Slavery, Manifest Destiny, the Holocaust, the Cultural Revolution…or the Killing Fields. For a while, it was called ethnic cleansing, or Genocide; currently it is called Jihad.

Oh, by the way, here in the 21th century, in America we now allow our citizens to arm themselves in a manner so they can kill great numbers of small children and/or grown-ups in a matter of minutes. We do this here in America by allowing our citizens to buy automatic weapons of modern war practically anytime they want. Then they shoot ten or twenty or thirty children or people in a movie theater, or a school, or in a church, or a night club.

"How could this be?" you could ask after so many have died. Here is one answer: *Many Americans are continuously willing to be killed rather than give up the right not to be.*

There is more than one way to kill off people. Now we just employ them *in a certain way*. It's like that song Roberta Flack made famous in 1973: "Killing Me Softly." Now we kill them off 'softly' by paying them in a manner that ensures perpetual poverty or does not include health care, or by offering them daily work activities in environments bad for their health or spirit, or we do not allow them paid time off for sick days or when their children are sick, or vacation time, and so on.

"Where do you work?" the man asked. He was just trying to be polite. He and the girl he was talking to were waiting for the bus. It was a gorgeous day: blue skies everywhere, birds singing, low humidity. They were waiting for the number 11 bus.

"At Walmart," said the young woman, adjusting her ponytail. She had a great voice, the man talking to her thought.

"Oh, I'm so sorry," said the man, who sincerely meant it. This happened a long time ago—back in 2009. The guy was a wise guy like me. In fact, it was me. I was in disguise, trying to gather material for what I hoped would soon be a famous book. At the moment, I was just like a Walmart employee—dreaming of becoming better off.

You Hold Your Index and Middle Finger up and Make a Fist.

IN WORLD WAR I, 116,000 American soldiers died—considerably fewer than the 600,000 soldiers who died right here during our Civil War just fifty years earlier. In less than twenty years from the end of World War I, World War was back in Europe. They called it World War II. This time, 416,000 US soldiers would die on the battlefields of Europe and Africa, on the beaches, in harbors, at sea, in the air, and on the islands of the South Pacific. Before the century was out, America would fight in two more fully fledged wars, a one-day event in the Caribbean, and a one-week action in the Middle East to prevent Iraq from invading Kuwait. In the fifties, over 25,000 American troops would die in the fight in North Korea; ten years later, some 58,000 more American soldiers would not make it out of Vietnam alive. All in all, in the twentieth century alone, the world had some eighty to ninety million *beings of incorrigible behavior and armed conflict* perish in wars and ethnic cleansings in Europe, North and South America, the South Pacific, Asia, Australia, and Africa. And, get this: historians will tell you that this was quite an improvement from previous centuries. Historians will tell you that. I'll tell you this: there were a lot of dead civilians and soldiers to play taps for.

Another thing we used to say often in the sixties was, "Peace." When boomers said peace, we raised up two fingers in a V-sign to show to the person we said it to. We used the index finger and the middle finger. This sign was first used in World War II to communicate victory. Boomers used this same hand gesture to communicate peace and to protest the war in Vietnam.

In the twentieth and early twenty-first centuries, in spite of what the historians will tell you, peace was more elusive than an *honest* Wall Street banker. By the year 2001, the sixties saying "Make love, not war!" was so much a part of our past it was like seeing the light from tiny sparkling stars in the night sky, sent hundreds of millions of years earlier.

"So, Paul, what's your number?" I didn't really know Paul very well. We were at college, in line for lunch. It was called the C-Shop. If you missed lunch in the cafeteria, you could go to the C-Shop. Both of us had missed the lunch served in the cafeteria. He was in my entering freshman class in the fall of 1967, two years ago. That year, we lived in the Presidents, a group of small dormitories just for freshman on the central campus. Paul was from Michigan. Like me, he had long hair and wore cutoffs, blue jean jackets, and sometimes shoes.

"Five," Paul said. He shrugged when he said it.

"Fuck. Oh man. Dude, I'm so sorry," I said. "I didn't know."

He would be dead in twenty months. He stepped on a mine in a jungle. He was nineteen years old when they put what was left of him in that body bag.

Compound Interest

DURING THE LATE FIFTIES, MY sisters and I, along with most of our generation, were about to experience a rather stable adolescence—not a war or a depression like our parents before us. Many of us were about to attend high school and higher education instead of going off to work to help support the family, or to a war to support the country. Most of Europe and many parts of the rest of the world were either still in recovery from World War II or were just struggling to feed, clothe, and employ their own people. Many people in the world thought all Americans lived like kings and queens. By the fifties, compared to most everyone in the world, we did. We still are. For instance, I had my own bedroom. Even my dad did not have his own bedroom growing up—nor did his brothers, nor any of his friends. Most children in the rest of the world did not have their own bedrooms. They still don't. The standard of living in the United States was so high that people in most other countries had to work many years to make what some Americans made in one year. Sometimes in one week. Sometimes in one day. It was so high you could say we were the Himalayas of income.

But get this: by 2012, in some poorer countries, it would take a person about thirty thousand years to earn the amount some of the big shots on Wall Street earn in just one year. Did you say thirty thousand, Dick? Yes, I did.

One day in 2014, in the *New York Times* business section, a reporter asked a rich guy, "How many homes do you have?"

"You want me to count?" he said.

"Yes," said the reporter.

"OK. I have an apartment in New York City, on Fifth Avenue across from the park. Of course there's Southampton. I paid cash for that one. I have North Salem in Westchester; I have Fisher Island in Florida; I have one where I go bird and quail hunting in Florida, too; and then there's Nantucket Island. Last, of course, there's Vail. My family and I ski. I paid cash for that one, too," he said sheepishly.

So one August day in the late fifties, my mother decided my sisters and I all needed new school clothes. My father, always the saver, requested that she forgo new clothes this year as she had been purchasing new school clothes for us at the end of each summer since before the Mayflower landed.

"Evelyn," he said, "I'm a little short this year. Can we see if the children can use their existing clothing?" My mother, always the spender, promised she would not use her charge account cards. Instead, he learned, she raided the savings accounts he was using to teach his three children the value of saving a little money each week. He was going to show us how saving a small amount each week would eventually add up to a much bigger amount if you kept it in the savings account. He was teaching us fiscal discipline. He was teaching us fiscal management. He was teaching us about compound interest. It was a good try. She cleaned out the accounts in five minutes. She bought the new clothes for cash—so much for his good idea.

He was beside himself. He yelled. He screamed. He threatened to divorce her. Standing there in her PJs and bare feet, not five feet away, was little Donna Caplan, my big sister and their oldest daughter. She was eleven. She was standing on the second step of the stairway that led to the bedroom she shared with my sister Sherry. She was witnessing this awful fight, and in spite of being eleven—or because of it—she explained to them right there in the kitchen that they would have to figure out some other solution. "Because," said the eleven-year-old, in these very words, "divorce is not an option."

Sweet versus Far Out

MOST OF MY PEERS WERE going to experience something called adolescence, a somewhat new phenomenon for the masses. Adolescence: a time period that for many of us was not dominated by leaving high school and seeking full-time employment for the necessities of life. In fact, for many of us, this moment would be dominated by non-necessities. There were so many of us. Many families were doing well enough during the late fifties and sixties that we quickly became a mini-economic force with part-time jobs and a small disposable income. There were so many of us that in the years to come we would turn into a major economic force that would last our whole lifetimes—even as old farts in the twenty-first century. We don't buy records anymore. But some of us did save our old vinyl ones. Oh, those album covers. Even if you did not save those, you still have records these days: medical records.

Now we download music and buy medical treatment. And of course, we are still buying drugs. Now it is not to provide chemically generated enthusiasm. This time it is to live longer. Oddly enough, the only similarities are the side effects. They all still cause running noses, diarrhea, upset stomachs, constipation, blurred vision, poor sleep, muscle aches, heart attacks, and significant loss of economic resources.

I worked during high school, but I did not have to. I mean *I had to*, but I didn't really have to. I worked in my dad's supermarket. I bagged groceries. I cleaned machines and made hamburger. On one Fourth of July, I made hamburger nonstop from seven thirty in the morning until two in the afternoon. I delivered groceries. I washed the meat room walls, the butcher blocks, and the floors, all for a buck an hour.

Imagine—for the first time, not just adolescents, but adolescents with disposable income. Imagine millions of them. "Far out," they said. "Far out" I said. My twenty-year-old son does not say, "Far out." He says, "Sweet." All his friends say, "Sweet." His name is Tom, just like his grandfather, whom he is partly named after. Karen had a favorite uncle named Tom and he is named after her uncle as well. He is nice, just like his grandfather; everyone says so.

My daughter doesn't say, "Far out!" For enhanced enthusiasm, she says, "Totally!" She is seven years older than my son. When she makes a point or wants to communicate a complicated issue, she says, "I totally get it!" She is like her brother. She is nice, too, and very smart like her mom. She is pretty, too.

In the mid-sixties, I put away my paycheck for college, for the movies, for a set of drums, and for gas to put into my parent's car so I could take out the girls who rang my dad's cash registers; the gasoline cost thirty cents a gallon.

Thirty years earlier, during the Depression, many of our fathers, then young boys, worked, too. They worked for dimes and quarters or a meal. Some worked all day for a meal. "Swell!" they said, and "t'anks, missta."

And now, for the first time ever in America, young women in droves (not just the upper class or royalty) were about to attend the same colleges and graduate schools as boys and change the world forever. They were going to demand equal opportunity and equal pay in the man's world of employment. My *own* sisters were going to demand equal pay. Most men had decided that women were second-rate employees and should be paid accordingly. The women were not having any more of that crap. This was not 1941, the last time in America when women had gone to work in droves. At that time, they were needed because all the men had gone off to war in Europe and the South Pacific. The war came, and the women were invited to work. Then that war ended, and they were shown the door.

This time was different. This time they wanted to use their education, their training. And this time, more than anything, they also wanted equal opportunity, equal pay, and equal justice in the work place. Now, some forty years later, some progress has been made, but they are still fighting.

1955–1961, Simpson Elementary School

IN 1960, THE COUNTRY ELECTED the youngest president ever. I debated Ron Jones in Mr. Thompson's sixth-grade class at Simpson Elementary School—that same Simpson Elementary School in which I'd previously spent so much time under my desk. Simpson School is gone now, of course. So is Mr. Thompson. I don't know about Ron.

In 2010, the developer finished the forty two-bedroom condos that had been erected on the old Simpson School site. Kathy Clark, my first girlfriend—who lived three houses down on Long Hill Road and had the big brother who scared the poop out of me—happened to be visiting her aunt, her mom's sister. Her aunt now lived in Kathy's childhood home. After college, Kathy had married and settled in Vermont. She and I took the very same walk down Long Hill Road we took so many times so many years ago. Simpson School was still there, but it was being taken down. At the site, we each took some bricks. They were all over the place. Kathy gave one to her brother. I gave one to my friend Tarn, from second grade. I have known Tarn forever. Mrs. Sebastian was the second-grade teacher's name. She had great toys at the back of her room, and I can say without hesitation that kind of made second grade for me.

Kathy and I fell in love the moment we laid eyes on each other. We were probably six years old. It has been a great love over the years. I have a picture of us when we were about seven years old. We are in our cowboy and cowgirl outfits (actually that is us on the book cover). I have six-shooters in both sides of my holster. I have suspenders holding up my cowboy pants over my cowboy shirt. I am not sure why I was wearing a cowboy shirt as my pants practically come up to my throat. We both had cowboy hats and cowboy boots on. If I'd stood any straighter, you would have thought I was trying to be a marine, not a cowboy. Kathy, on the other hand, looks as cute as a button. What a face! What a smile!

One night in the early seventies, we both happened to be in town at the same time. We had not seen each other in years. We were now in our early twenties. We drank some wine and slept together. For a New York minute, we thought it was love. In the morning, when we woke up, it took us less than a second to realize we were supposed to be brother and sister, not that other boy-girl stuff. I woke up, and I said to her, "I didn't know!"

She said right back to me, "Neither did I!"

I am told that "phase one" of the Simpson School condo site is sold out. In 1960, if you said the word "condo," no one would have known what in the heck you were talking about. During the fall of 1960, on this future site of these condos, in front of the class, Ron Jones and I were debating who would make a better president of the United States. Ronnie had Mr. Nixon, and I had Mr. Kennedy. We debated. The class voted. I won. Mr. Kennedy made it easy for me.

Little did I know, but that same Mr. Kennedy shopped in my dad's supermarket, right there in *The Building* he had bought on North Main Street. In 1934 and 1935, John F. Kennedy was attending Choate. He bought candy. He bought soda. He bought gum. Choate was less than a half mile up the road on North Main Street. Usually, the first stop for students coming from the school was Caplan's Supermarket for snacks, candy, and soft drinks. And get this: in 1935, when John F. Kennedy graduated, he was voted most likely to succeed.

October 14, 1890—Birth Date of Dwight D. Eisenhower

HE WAS BORN IN THE fall of 1890, fourteen years before my father. He led our troops to victory in Europe in World War II. He helped get rid of that maniac in Germany. He planned D-day, code name Operation Overlord. In 1911, he graduated from West Point. When he graduated, my dad was seven years old. He was clearly one of the good guys—a gentleman. And in 1952, he was elected president of the United States. He beat Adlai Stevenson, another gentleman. In 1951, two gentlemen ran for president. In my lifetime, I am not sure it has ever happened since.

General Eisenhower was a war hero. In the fifties, he promised to end the war in Korea. He ran as a Republican. Then he won. Then he *did* end that war. I'll tell you one thing. If you want to end a war, sometimes it's better to put a general—a warrior—in the office of president when America is at war.

There was no way he would lose. Everyone liked Ike. Remember the campaign button everyone was wearing? It said, "I like Ike."

He kept all of President Roosevelt's New Deal. He desegregated the armed forces. He sent federal troops to Little Rock, Arkansas, to integrate the public schools. He had the federal government fund our new expanded highway system. He warned us of the military-industrial complex. He would not support Senator Joe McCarthy's paranoia about communists. Basically, he was an intelligent, well-balanced man who employed intellectual thought, and—when politics would allow—common sense. He even played golf. He was a Republican president any American—any Democrat—could admire. He served two terms.

If this leader, this Republican, this general, this fellow Eisenhower were in office today, the Tea Party folks and other Republicans would try and have him removed for being a socialist.

"My Mouth Doesn't Work That Way," I said.

ERNEST HEMINGWAY DIED ON JULY 2, 1961. He was sixty-one years old. My dad was fifty-seven. I was twelve. At the time, I did not have a clue whom Hemingway was. I was studying for my bar mitzvah, the Jewish coming-of-age ceremony which would occur in nine months, on my thirteenth birthday. I had to learn Hebrew prayers in order to chant them aloud for everyone at the Saturday morning service. I hated it. It was impossible to learn. I told the rabbi, "My mouth doesn't work that way."

I came to literature late in life. "Why read the book when you can see it in the movies?" I was talking to Billy James, an eleven year old friend at Simpson school. We were discussing the book The Swiss Family Robinson by Johann David Wyss. Billy had just read it and loved it. Disney had just released a movie version. My opinion would change years later. When I was in college in Yellow Springs, Ohio, I wanted desperately to become another Ernest Hemingway: you know, a young writer, adventurous, famous, and sometimes rich. Actually, except for the young part, I still do. I read him until there was nothing else he wrote left to read.

In the sixties and early seventies, I wrote short stories and sometimes poetry. I even won some awards. I wrote about Freddy Frog and Marsha Mosquito and how they fell in love down off Friday Avenue in a place called Saturday Afternoon Swamp. I wrote about Weathering

59

Wind and Otchie-Potchie Land and the children who lived there. They all had funny names like Mostly Music Mary, Lonely Larry Lettuce, or Too Tall Terry. Long ago, when I was very little, my oldest sister Donna told me stories about Otchie-Potchie Land at bedtime. She made them up. She was pretty good at it. She makes up stories still. She has to—she has five grandsons! Perhaps later I will tell you about Freddy Frog. He is quite the character. He lives in Saturday Afternoon Swamp, right off Friday Avenue near Otchie-Potchie Land.

The Movie Was in Color, but the Movie Theater Was in Black-and-White

I THINK IT WAS 1966, the summer before my junior year in high school. I was just sixteen. I had just gotten my driver's license and was still dreaming of touching naked breasts. I was working in my dad's supermarket and taking a summer math course at Choate, the famous private high school in Wallingford. I was trying to improve my skills for the math college board I would take in my junior year of high school.

I met her in math class. It took me the entire summer to get the courage up to talk to her. Her name was Carolyn. She told me she was from Gainesville, Georgia. I liked her right off the bat. She was very pretty, and so nice. She had a smile that could make a boy like me feel like he'd just been run over by a hundred-thousand-pound tractor. By the end of a summer of math at Choate, I drove that Georgia peach from Choate to my home about one mile away. We made out in the living room, listening to Ray Charles and Frank Sinatra. She was wonderful. The night was full of soft music, first romance, kissing, and touching—and later that night, aching feelings in my pants. She was leaving Wallingford in a few days. The summer program was ending.

The next day, it was my father who told me. I was to go see the teacher who ran the Choate summer program and apologize to him.

Carolyn and I had broken the rules. I didn't know. No overnight students were ever to leave the campus without permission from the administration. This particular date of ours was hardly a secret. I had told my parents, but no matter. I was to go to the campus and apologize to this administrator. It was my father's idea. My father was instructing me on how to be an adult. I went. I apologized. The only question I worried about was if they were going to let me see Carolyn again. School was over in a day, and all the students would be leaving. I had to see her. I did not even have her address. Her kisses had me in a spell.

"I'll write you," she said. "You have to write back."

"I will write," I said. "When do you leave?"

"Tomorrow." She looked like she was going to cry and it made me feel like crying, too. I told her I didn't know how, but I would visit her in Georgia. "I really will."

It would be almost two years before I saw her again. I would hitchhike to her home in Georgia from Yellow Springs, Ohio. It was to be an adventure. I was in college now, and I was taking a little road trip. I would attend what I called "on the road" classes for a bit.

I don't think her father knew what to make of me. I hardly looked like any college student he knew of. I had shown up my best north of the Mason-Dixie line counterculture outfit. But he tolerated me and even let me drive his speedboat. Carolyn and I drove that boat out to an island in this gigantic lake (man-made, I think), and once again I got to kiss those lips that had caused such a stir two years ago.

That night, we decided to go to the movies. We went to see *In the Heat of the Night*. We went to downtown Gainesville, Georgia, and went right to that movie theater and bought some popcorn. The movie starred the black actor Sidney Poitier as a self-assured, competent, big-city police detective from the North. It also starred the white actor Rod Steiger, who portrayed a racist southern sheriff who was at the moment in over his head trying to solve a recent murder in his little southern town. The timeline in the movie and the current time were identical: the late sixties.

The movie theater was integrated, if you want to call it that. The African Americans sat up in the balcony. The whites sat below. During the movie, when the balcony cheered, the whites below were silent. When the whites below cheered, the balcony was silent. At the end of the movie, the black detective from the North solves the crime for the sheriff. The racist sheriff appears to come to respect the black detective. At the end of the movie, in Gainesville, Georgia, there was applause from the black balcony. The white folks below, quiet as church mice, filed out with their heads lowered.

The Black Panthers

IN THE LATE SIXTIES, THE Black Panthers caught the attention of most of the students on campus at Antioch College. At Antioch, there was a small dormitory for students who wanted to speak only French; there was another for students who wanted only to speak Spanish. These were experiments in learning a language. One day, a black student proposed an all-black dormitory. It was an experiment, too. They wanted a dormitory that just spoke "black."

It also caught the attention of the US government. The government did not think much of this experiment and sent letters to the college saying that it was breaking federal law. The college and its students were in jeopardy of losing their funding from the federal college loan programs. As at most colleges, many students at Antioch participated in those programs. The law they were referring to said a college could not *segregate* dormitories by race. It was very clear on this issue. In fact, it was a similar law that sent federal troops into Mississippi and Alabama years before to guarantee that a couple of black students be admitted to the all-white universities and housed in their all-white dormitories, fed in their all-white cafeterias, and schooled in their all-white classrooms.

Soon Antioch College closed its all-black dormitory. Some black students were caught in the middle of this issue. My best friend at the time, Nardie, transferred to Boston University because of it. He was black, and his crime was living with a white student: me. One day, he told me he had been 'spoken to'. Spoken to? He did not argue. It would be pointless, and he knew it. Black men no longer dated white women. Black women no longer dated white men. Black students no longer lived with their white friends. It was a sad and fearful time for everyone. One day there was the celebration of integration, the next day, the constant weight of self-imposed segregation.

In some cities, the Black Panthers provided day care in poor neighborhoods. Sometimes they provided self-concept or self-esteem programs to young black children. Sometimes they provided food. Sometimes they provided protection. White people had the police to protect them. White people had a government to protect them. In certain parts of our country, if black people wanted to be safe, they had to learn how to be invisible.

In the early seventies, a judge in New Haven, Connecticut, would surprise everyone and throw one of the cases of Black Panthers on trial for murder out of court. One case was against the founder of the Black Panthers, Bobby Seale. While I was taking college courses in psychology and English in Ohio, someone was trying to pin a murder charge on him in New Haven, Connecticut. Some thought it was J. Edgar Hoover.

In 1970, I was twenty-one. Bobby Seale was thirty-four. J. Edgar Hoover was seventy-five.

Whenever possible, I was living with the very smart pretty girl who had bangs and long brown hair, and a dimple in the middle of her chin who wanted to marry me most of the time. She was twenty-one years old, too.

In New Haven, the Panther named Warren Kimbro was convicted of torturing and murdering another Black Panther for supposedly feeding information to the FBI. Mr. Kimbro and the leader of the New Haven chapter of the Black Panthers both turned state's evidence in exchange for a lesser charge. In 2006, thirty-six years after he was convicted of murder and sentenced to life in prison, and thirty-two years following his release, he was working in New Haven for the social service agency Project More. In fact he had been running this agency for the Department of Corrections since the eighties. In 1972, two years after being sent to prison for murder, the parole board had allowed Warren to attend Harvard University. He was subsequently released from prison four years following his incarceration. He had been serving a life sentence. How come he was released after serving only four years for being a convicted murderer? Many people in New Haven still wonder about that. What did the Department of Correction or the judge know that the rest of us did not?

Was the poor black kid from Florida who relocated to New York City, who then joined the Black Panthers, who was sent from New York City to the New Haven Panthers 'set up' by the FBI. People "in the know" thought that "talking to the FBI" was *misinformation* put "on the street" by the FBI to disrupt the New Haven office of the Black Panther organization. Apparently, the FBI had done this kind of thing elsewhere.

Warren Kimbro, the ex-Panther and ex-felon, ran Project MORE, a day treatment and halfway house program for prisoners funded by the Department of Correction. Around 2006, Project MORE and Columbus House, the agency where I worked, were selected to keep newly released young convicts from New Haven from returning to prison faster than you could say "recidivism." It was a Re-entry Program. I used to do that kind of stuff. I'll tell you about it later.

Long Hill Road

IN THE FIFTIES, MY LIFE was a series of games played outside by the children of Long Hill Road, run by the children of Long Hill Road, created by the children of Long Hill Road, and refereed by the children of Long Hill Road. It was not a supervised moment. It was not an adult moment. Unless it was raining or someone's birthday, the adults were at work or inside houses. We were outside.

"You wanna play cowboys and Indians?" I asked. I was speaking to Kathy, Skipper, Joanie, and Leila: the usual Long Hill Road gang. We were in my backyard. It was the summer of 1956. The sky was so blue you would have thought it was a Caribbean Ocean.

"No," Leila said. "I'm not playing that." Leila was "all-girl" and not inclined to play games if they included the possibility of running, falling, jumping, climbing, or even screaming. She was very dainty. She had jet-black hair and always wore pretty outfits. Even as a little girl, she mostly knew what she wanted and had little trouble verbalizing it.

"I'll play," said Kathy. She was game for almost anything. And she already had her cowgirl outfit on. Few things would slow her down. She and I were inseparable for a while back then in the midfifties.

Skipper said, "I'll play. I'm going to be the Lone Ranger."

"I'm going be Dale Rogers," said Joanie.

Leila turned and stormed up the street back to her house without saying another word.

The selection of games or teams was performed by children. Rules were established and upheld by children. All referees were children. Play was simple. The only real observer was Lassie, a collie who was in fact a dead ringer for the TV dog. Lassie lived with Kathy. Kathy lived three houses down the hill with her brother, her mom and dad, and her mom's parents. Her brother David was several years older than us, big and strong. I was frightened of him. Much of life confused me, but I was clear about David. I was scared of him, all right. Exactly why, I could not say. Fortunately, he rarely played with us.

Skipper, on the other hand, was bigger and older than me, but he did not frighten me. He had an easygoing style that was never confrontational. He lived up the hill in a house that always smelled like sauerkraut. We played army together almost daily during the summertime, across the street on the first hole of the Wallingford Country Club. Our play was occasionally interrupted by the call to food, rest, Hebrew school, homework or bedtime by an adult voice, a horn, or sometimes even by a cowbell.

In the winter, we rode our sleds on that golf course. We raced those sleds; those American Flyers. We soaped the metal sled runners for speed. If the sled was big enough, we sat behind each other or we laid down and stacked ourselves on top of one another. Then we raced down the hills, often crashing into each other's sleds just for fun. Someone would always bring a "flying saucer," or sometimes just a big old rubber tire tube. Of course we would build a jump half way down the hill.

In the summer, the winter race tracks turned into army battle-fields or cowboy shootouts. We got pretend shot; sometimes we got killed. Sometimes we got captured, and sometimes we got put in jail.

In the spring, we celebrated warmth and the freedom from layers of jackets, snow pants, boots, hats, and gloves. When the golfers were not on the course, we performed incredible acts of bravery and strength during imaginary battles of life and death.

On the hottest days of summer, we trucked up the street through the backyards until we came to the Downey mansion. It had an in-ground pool in the backyard, and occasionally, we were given permission to swim in that pool. Mrs. Downey's black butler would often bring us Cokes to drink. Mrs. Downey was the sister of Morton Downey, a famous singer during the thirties and forties and father of the radio talk-show host Morton Downey, Jr. In the eighties, Morton Downey Jr. set the standards for all the right-wing radio talk shows that would come in the future. His radio station was in Sacramento, California. He was fired in 1983 for telling a racist joke. Guess who replaced him: Rush Limbaugh!

We stayed up later in the summertime, and I could stay outside forever. In the fall, I would mourn the end of summer, the return to school, and the early darkness that descended on us all. The four seasons came and went, and the weather changes in the seasons and sports structured my life: Little League in the spring, camp in the summer, football in the fall, then in the winter, basketball, sledding, ice skating on ponds, and teaching myself to ski on the gentle slopes of the golf course across the street.

In December, we celebrated the Santa part of Christmas. We were Jewish, but Santa came to our house, too. Actually, we celebrated both Chanukah and Christmas. No Christmas tree, but stockings and plenty of presents by the fireplace on Christmas morn.

"I have something to tell you," my sister Donna said. I was seven years old. Donna was twelve. We were wrapping a present for our mother up in Donna and Sherry's room. Chanukah was over. Christmas was coming in a couple of days.

"I know what you're going to say," I replied. I knew that look she had. She was going to tell me something I would not like. "You are going to tell me he doesn't really exist, aren't you?"

"Yes."

"It's Mom and Dad, isn't it?"

"Yes." My sister Sherry was there, too. She already knew. She was three years older than me. She was staring at me to see how I would take it.

Shadows

OUR HOLIDAY MEALS ALMOST ALWAYS included some combination of my mother's relatives: my mother's parents, my great aunt Fannie and sometimes one of her girlfriends, my mom's younger brother and his family. In the early fifties, my mother's younger brother, Richard, asked my dad to be best man at his wedding. I told you, everyone really liked Tom. After Richard grew up, he was a history teacher in a public high school one town away from Wallingford. He is about twenty years older than me. One day he would become chairman of that history department. Moments later, he would retire to Florida. Like me, he would say this business of life would go as fast as Superman flies, all right.

All families are weird. Certainly ours was no different. The holiday meals on Long Hill Road did not include any other Caplans. In fact, I can only remember my dad's oldest brother Jake coming to visit once or twice. And then there was Sidney. He was a Harrison, the son of one of Dora's brothers from Springfield, Massachusetts. The brother's wife had died when Sidney was just a young boy. In the early twentieth century, Dora took in her brother's little boy, as her brother could not raise Sidney alone. Sidney was younger than Tom. Eventually he went to work for Tom as a butcher and stayed a lifetime.

I do not remember my dad's younger brother Itzie, or Itzie's wife, Ida ever being in our house. When I was a baby, my sisters tell me, they came often. Ida and her daughter, Debbie, came too. Debbie was exactly Sherry's age. In the forties, Itzie and his family lived uptown on North Main Street in a two-family house Tom had bought right in the heart of the fancy old Yankee neighborhood. No more living across from the railroad yards for the Caplans. Itzie, Ida, and Debbie lived upstairs, and my grandparents, together with Jake's wife Beatrice and their children, lived downstairs.

Itzie ran the store downtown at the bottom of Center Street, and Tom ran the big new remodeled store in *The Building* on Main Street. Within a few years, Tom would close the store downtown and double the size of the uptown store. He would bring Itzie uptown to work in what America had recently begun referring to as a *supermarket*: a very large food store that sold produce, meats, fish, frozen foods, dry goods, housewares, home supplies, and groceries. Here was the new concept: it was self-service. You now got a small trolley (cart) as you walked into the store, and then you took the items you wanted right off the shelves, placing them into the cart. No more giving an employee a list of what you wanted. When you were finished, you pushed the cart to the checkout counter, where an employee emptied the items from your cart, "rang up" the order, and then put them into bags for you to carry or drive home with. If you had a car, another employee would push the cart out to the car and put them in for you.

Once the Center Street store closed Itzie came up to manage this new big supermarket. Itzie would arrive early each morning to open it and left each evening promptly at closing time. As their mother had asked him, Tom was taking good care of his younger brother. In the late twenties, he had sent him to Tufts University. Itzie played basketball for them. College did not work out for Itzie, so he came back home. Tom put him to work in the store. They were each to earn the same salary. Years later, he gave him 40 percent of everything: the food store, the real estate, and eventually stocks and bonds. Itzie would open the store. Tom did everything else.

But one winter during the midfifties, while Tom and Evelyn were vacationing in Florida, Ida, Itzie's wife, had come to the store and made an unusual request to Claire.

All through her high school years, Claire had been Tom's waitress at the Emerald Restaurant in uptown Wallingford. It was around the corner from the new Caplan's Market on North Main Street. Tom and other Caplan Market employees ate there often or took their coffee breaks there.

She would teach him Hungarian words, and he would teach her Russian or Yiddish ones as she waited on him. He loved it. She had a sparkle and a gentle way with people he was looking for in the management of his growing real estate company. Now she was calling Tom in Florida after Ida had made the request.

"TOM?" Claire asked. She spoke into the phone louder than usual, as she was on the telephone calling a place very, very far away from Wallingford: Florida. At the time, many people did this when they called "long distance." At the time, she was in her mid-twenties. Years ago, when she'd graduated high school, Tom had asked her to come and work for him to keep the books for his growing real estate company. His accountant would train her. She would grow into the position of managing most of the women who worked full and part-time in the offices of both Caplan's Market and the real estate. In Wallingford, this was a choice job for a woman with no formal training.

"Claire, is something wrong?" Tom asked, hearing distress in her voice.

"Ida brought her brother-in-law here today—the one from New Jersey. She had me give him all the supermarket and real estate accounting books. Tom, I didn't know what to do. I gave them to him. I'm so sorry." She continued speaking very loud.

"Claire, you did the right thing. I'll deal with this when I get back." He told her not to worry. Then he thanked her for calling and hung up.

He told Claire not to do anything. What happened after he returned from Florida, I will never know, but I can tell you that Itzie and Ida never again stepped into our house again.

I always thought Itzie was a hard man. He was short in stature, quick in tongue, and lacked people skills. He would fire workers who questioned him or employees he did not like, and then Tom would rehire them after he got back from lunch. Tom made all the decisions. Itzie was along for the ride. Itzie lived in Tom's shadow, but it was a comfortable one.

During the fifties and sixties, while Claire balanced cash registers at the end of each day, worked on the real estate books, or delivered my sisters to dance school or piano lessons, Tom would stay at the store after it closed and make out the ads or think about new investments. He might also "check the heat," code between Claire and Tom for getting drinks next door at the Tip Top Bar & Grill with friends who popped in after closing time. Claire would come to work at noon and stay long after the store closed. She ran the office. She paid his bills and managed his real estate. She started working for him in 1948. In1974, after his death, she continued to work for me until the fall of 2011. That's right, over sixty years.

Claire's parents had a little corner grocery store in their neighborhood, half a mile away from Tom's big store on North Main Street. When Claire's father got sick, in the late fifties, Tom would send Claire home to care for him and tell her to stay there until he got better. He invented family leave before the smart folks in Washington, DC, did. Claire would never forget. Tom sent employees from his big supermarket to run little neighborhood corner stores for owners he knew in Wallingford if they or their families got sick, too. He would not forget his roots. He would not forget that he was a small-town guy. He did not forget where he came from or how immigrants from Russia and elsewhere in Europe took care of each other.

The Caplans would take care of my Uncle Jake's children, a boy and a girl, and Jake's wife, Beatrice, after Jake left Wallingford and relocated to New York City. These children loved Tom. I know this because they've told me so. On the other hand, Itzie's wife, Ida, never trusted Tom. If she thought she could turn her husband away from his brother, she was mistaken. Tom let Ida hate him all she wanted. Itzie would let her, too, but he still cared for his brother.

Other than our love for Tom Caplan and our last names, my uncle Itzie and I only had one thing in common. In Wallingford, I lived in Tom's shadow, too—a different kind, but still a shadow. When I leave Wallingford, there is no shadow.

I have a full-page Caplan's Supermarket ad from the local newspaper, dated April 1, 1932. I put it in a frame. It's hanging in my office. The full-page ad announced Tom Caplan's grand-opening sale for his new-concept supermarket. Tom Caplan would bring in a product no one else had yet: something called frozen foods. Strawberries in the wintertime! Peaches, too, it advertised. "The flavor is sealed in," it said. It was unheard of. Tom Caplan had brought Charlie Birdseye's new invention of frozen foods to Wallingford. Tom was practically the first in the state to have them. You could not just buy the product to sell. You, the store owner, had to buy the special cases—frozen-food cases—for the product to go in.

In the same ad, eggs were advertised at twenty-five cents a dozen. Coffee was twenty-six cents a pound. Butter was twenty-four cents a pound. Leg of lamb was just twenty-one cents a pound; a pound of center-cut swordfish was thirty-five cents, and a ten-pound sack of sugar went for thirty-nine. When people come to my office now and see the ad, they say, "Would you look at those prices!" A long time ago I used to say right back, "Can you dig it?"

Some twenty years later, during the 1950's, the women who worked in the supermarket office loved it when little children came in. They were well prepared, with little candies, coloring books, and a wall area that displayed the children's artwork. Often the little ones would be looking for Tom. He had lots of handholding buddies. My sisters and I, who often visited the store, were lectured by my father and mother to respect the staff and not to bother them. Itzie and Ida's daughter, Debbie, was more of a challenge for the staff. At the age of eight, she told them regularly, "My daddy owns this store." Then this eight-year-old would add, "You have to do what I say."

Old man

Old man is it possible to tell you how strong
Your soul shines in the heart of your son
Do you see his eyes sing when your face smiles?
Do you see his body dance to the sound
Of your laughter?

Be careful with your son.
He is only a boy who hasn't learned you are
Only a man with a past and a present.

Old man he is a boy who seeks to make your joy
Who is afraid to play his own music
Because his rhythms do not fit your tune
And his life is still too wrapped up in your show.

Listen old man – you have gifted your son with all
The goods of greed
But you have not soured his need to taste the
Truth of your seed.

You and your son perform a sad silent love affair
Speaking of each other to others with love and admiration
But face to face words stop locked in thoughts
And the feelings of a lifetime are stored until
The ears of a stranger can be found.

It is time for one of us to speak up-
There is love in my hand and it wishes to shake yours.

Winter 1971

A Rhodes Scholar, or It's a Small World After All

IN THE SIXTIES, JOSEPH HELLER wrote *Catch-22*, a funny book about World War II. One of my favorite authors, Kurt Vonnegut Jr., wrote one too—*Slaughterhouse-Five*. In the fifties, John Wayne played a strong and brave foot soldier in a World War II movie, *The Sands of Iwo Jima*. Then, in the sixties, he played an equally strong but now smart and very strategic general in a movie about the Vietnam War, *The Green Berets*. No one made movies about the Korean War.

Years earlier, in the fifties, J. D. Salinger published a book about prep schools and phonies. Did you know he had worked on *The Catcher in the Rye* for ten years before it was published?

In 1960, Harper Lee published *To Kill a Mockingbird,* a book about growing up in the deep South during the thirties, and about justice or the lack of it for black people. In, the 1962 movie version, Gregory Peck played Atticus Finch, the lawyer who defended the black man accused of rape. Many of us either fell in love with Mr. Peck or wanted to get some advice from him after seeing that movie. Meanwhile, that Robert Zimmerman fellow from Hibbing, Minnesota—a.k.a. Dylan—wrote folk songs that inspired a generation not to settle for the status quo and suggested we take another look at the behavior of our current American politicians, our military, and our big corporations.

Sherry Caplan, the soon-to-be architect and my other older sister, would eventually marry another architect, who also came from Hibbing, Minnesota and graduated high school with that Robert Zimmerman guy. After high school and college, this smart Irishman would become a Rhodes Scholar. And like that Dylan fellow, his classmate, he too would travel the world making a living displaying, inventing, and negotiating his art.

Before Drugs: Wonder Boy

DURING THE LATE FIFTIES, AT nine years of age, I often used to day-dream of running outside, looking up, catching the atomic bomb dropped on us by the evil communists with my own bare hands, and thus saving the world. See the headlines: The Boy Who Saved the Planet. Wonder Boy—that was me. No kidding.

Years later, of course, some of us became more interested in peace and love. We saw the pictures of Hiroshima and Nagasaki. Perhaps as we got older, getting under a small desk in a school building next to windows bigger than a B-52 bomber, when someone dropped an atom bomb near you was not adding up. Peace and love certainly seemed a reasonable alternative to an atomic World War III.

Wonder Boy had his sixth birthday party in the backyard. It was April, and the sun was shining and warming us up, reminding us of what last summer was like. Leila was there. My sisters were there. Skipper was there. Kathy was there. So was Joanie, Kathy's cousin. Kathy and Joanie had given me small but real garden tools for a present: a child-size red hoe, a green rake, and a brown shovel. Soon after I opened the present, Joanie and I would debate who would use the hoe first. During the debate, she reintroduced me to the hoe by smashing it on my nose. I cried and was taken to Dr. Boyd's office. Dr. Boyd was our family doctor. When I was a boy, if my sisters or I were sick enough to stay in bed, we did not go to his office. Dr. Boyd would come to our house to see us.

At the office that day, I arrived with a bleeding cut on my nose. Dr. Boyd called his nurse to come in and clean the wound up and bandage it. No stiches were necessary. Poor Dr. Boyd's nurse. In those days, Dr. Boyd's nurse was Joanie's mother.

"Mr. President, you certainly cannot say that Dallas doesn't love you," said Nellie Connally, the wife of the governor of Texas. Moments later, President Kennedy was shot in the head and killed while riding in an open limo with her, her husband, John, the governor, and the President's own wife, Jackie, on the streets of Dallas, Texas.

THE FIRST SHOT I READ about was fired on June 12, 1963. I was fourteen. It was fired from an Enfield 1917 rifle. The man who was shot staggered from his driveway some thirty feet and then collapsed. The driveway was in Mound Bayou, Mississippi. They took him to the local hospital in Jackson, but he was refused admission because he was black. His name was Medgar Evers. He was thirty-seven years old. He was a known civil rights activist. He was a NAACP leader who was raising racial issues that made many whites in Mississippi angry. He was eventually admitted to that hospital and died some fifty minutes later. I did not understand.

"Why would that white guy shoot him?" I asked. Someone told me the answer. "Because he was black" they said.

"Why?" I asked again. I didn't get it the second time it was explained either.

Medgar Evers was a veteran of World War II who had survived D-Day on the shores of Normandy. He was buried in Arlington National Cemetery, with full honors. More than three thousand people attended. He was a married father of three. He had survived Normandy, but he could not survive Mound Bayou, Mississippi.

I would work that summer in my father's supermarket. I would bag groceries and take them out to cars. Sometimes I rounded up carts. I would sweep floors, empty trash, stack boxes. Sometimes I would help stock shelves. My favorite job was to go out all over town with our delivery man in the store's 1960 Chevy van and help him carry the groceries into the houses.

Two weeks after Medgar Edgar was shot, Bryon Dela Beckwith, a white man, was arrested and charged with his murder. I was mildly aware of this. I was not aware that an all-white jury deadlocked—twice—on a verdict. I know now that thirty-one years later, in 1994, he was tried again on new evidence. This time he was convicted and sentenced to prison. He died in prison in 2001, at the age of eighty.

This was not America's first murder of a civil rights activist. This was just one generation's introduction to the horror of racially driven events, of racial inequality in the courts, and of the racial realities that black people endured every day in certain areas in America. Many young white people in America were soon to discover that justice for black people, as it had for Medgar Evers, always took a very long time.

Two months later, on September 15, 1963, four young black girls—one eleven years old and the other three fourteen—were attending Sunday school in Alabama when they were murdered by a KKK member named Robert E. Chambliss and several others. In the fall of 1963, I was fourteen years old, too. I was entering prep school in New Jersey.

While I was still sleeping in my bed at the Blair Academy prep school in Blairstown, New Jersey, Robert E. Chambliss and some other Klansmen in Birmingham, Alabama, put sticks of dynamite with a timer under the steps of the all-black Sixteenth Street Baptist Church. Here is how justice worked in Birmingham, Alabama, on my mother's birthday, October 8, in 1963: for killing those children attending Sunday school, Robert Chambliss was found innocent; Mr. Chambliss was pronounced guilty of possession of dynamite (he did not have a permit) and had to pay a hundred-dollar fine and serve six months in prison. Regarding black people, the courts in Alabama worked much like the courts of Mississippi.

But that was not the end of it. In 1971, eight years later, the attorney general of Alabama reopened the case. He requested files regarding this incident from the FBI. Whose files? The files were from the Director of the FBI, J. Edgar Hoover. In a 1965 memo, Hoover names four people responsible for this incident: "Dynamite Bob," as Mr. Chambliss was known, and three others who had been identified by the FBI as possible suspects. At the time of the first trial, Hoover—then director of the FBI—had withheld all this information from the prosecutors in Alabama. In 1977, Chambliss was retried for murdering those girls, found guilty of four murders and sent to prison for many lifetimes. Mr. Chambliss died in prison in 1985. He was eighty-one years old. Three others connected to the crime were arrested in 2001. Two more were brought to trial and convicted of murder. One was found to be mentally incompetent. This time, it took justice thirty-eight years to find itself.

The next shot was fired five months later, on the morning of November 22, 1963. President John F. Kennedy was assassinated while riding in the backseat of an open limo on the streets of Dallas, Texas. He was forty-six years old. Like most of my peers, I was in school when he was shot. I was still fourteen years old. This time, we all noticed. I was a freshman attending a private high school in New Jersey. I was having a devil of a time fitting in there. It wasn't at all like overnight summer camp, as I'd imagined. At that moment, I was impatiently awaiting the Thanksgiving break. My parents both thought I'd be home for good before Christmas. Across the country, public and private schools were closing early out of respect for the fallen president.

Nine months after the church was blown up and seven months following the assassination of President Kennedy, on June 21, 1964, three young civil rights workers were arrested in a small Mississippi town and put in jail. No one could ever say what they were arrested for. I was now fifteen and had finished my freshman year in prep school. Earlier in the year, I had been so homesick I called home almost every other day.

"Operator, I need to make a collect call."

"Who should I say is calling?"

"Say it's from Dick," I replied. In the sixties, when you called "collect," you had to tell the operator who the call was from so the person who received it could decide whether to accept the charges.

But in Mississippi, on that June day, the jailer—a deputy sheriff, who had arrested the civil rights workers for reasons no one could ever find—would not allow them any phone calls, local or long distance. Instead of allowing them the one phone call each allowed by law, the sheriff called his buddies in the local KKK chapter. Civil rights workers called the jail to look for them. They were lied to and told they were not there. Later that night, the deputy at the jail let the arrested workers go, but while they were driving out of town, he stopped them again and held them on the side of the road. When the KKK arrived, they took them away, burned their car, dumped it in the swamp, and then tortured and murdered them. One worker was black, and two were white. Those two white young men were from New York. The young black man was from Mississippi. They were twenty, twenty-one, and twenty-four years old. They were there to help black people register to vote. That would be the last thing they would ever do.

The state of Mississippi refused to prosecute anyone for these murders. Eventually Bobby Kennedy, then the attorney general of the United States of America, sent the Department of Justice to prosecute eighteen men. All they managed to obtain were some guilty counts on much lesser charges. Some served from three to six years in prison. Soon movies were made about this event. Books were written. Apparently, everyone in the United States knew what happened to these young men except the courts of Mississippi.

In 2005, thirty-nine years later and thanks to the perseverance and due diligence of those who believed in the law, eighty-year-old Edgar Ray Killen, a longtime member of the KKK in Mississippi, was retried and convicted of three counts of murder. He is now serving three consecutive twenty-year prison terms.

In 2005, when Mr. Killen went to prison, forty-one years after the day of the event, I was fifty-four years old. I was working with the homeless at a social service agency called Columbus House in New Haven. It was close to where I was born, close to where my dad had driven an old model-T truck to pick up supplies for the little store in Wallingford, close to where my mother grew up, close to where those Yalies who dated my mother lived on campus, close to where my aunt made hats, and close to where those two Black Panthers had tortured another Black Panther for supposedly talking to the FBI.

Later in 1963, I would finally learn firsthand about prejudice. Some boys at school would say terrible things about Jewish people right to my face. It would upset me. But no one would put dynamite sticks with a timer under my bed or in an area where I was going to be. I wasn't fully attuned to quite what it was, but it was clear to me that something in the country was very wrong.

On February 21, 1965, a little over a year later, Malcolm X was shot to death by three members of a Muslim religious organization he used to belong to. I was now fifteen years old. I would be sixteen in less than two months. Much to my parents' surprise, I was still at that same private high school in New Jersey, now a sophomore. Recently, Malcolm X had found out there was more than one way to be a good Muslim. Apparently some other Muslims did not agree with him. He was thirty-nine when they shot him for practicing a variation of Islam.

We had religion class in this private Presbyterian prep school I was attending. They were big on religion. We had chapel every day but Wednesday and Saturday; on those days, we had sporting events with other prep schools. In 1966, I won the religion prize. In the four years I was there, no one ever talked informatively or formally about Islam.

Then, on April 4, 1968, just three years following the death of Malcom X, Martin Luther King was shot, assassinated while standing on a balcony of his motel room in Memphis, Tennessee. He was there advocating for the garbage workers. King admired Mahatma Gandhi, the leader of India's independence movement from the British in the 1920's through the 1940's. He was committed to fighting social, racial, or religious and economic discrimination with nonviolent civil disobedience. King and much of the civil rights movement utilized Gandhi's tactics. Edgar Hoover had the FBI keep a close eye on King. Following Reverend King's assassination, black residents of over one hundred American cities took to the streets to riot, burn, and loot. America was on fire.

I was five days away from being nineteen. I was older now and more aware of the world I lived in. I was now in college. In June of 1972, Martin Luther King's wife, Coretta, would speak at my graduation. In the mid-forties, she had attended Antioch College herself. She had gone on a full scholarship, as did two other black girls. After her husband was shot dead for advocating for the poor, for the middle class, and for black people through nonviolence, Hoover would put Mrs. King under surveillance, too. She was a widow and a mother of four committed to nonviolence, peace, and democracy—oh yea, surely a dangerous woman.

In the late forties, Antioch College had begun integrating the campus. You could say without much hesitation that in spite of all of its financial problems, in some areas, Antioch College was lightyears ahead of its time.

The next shooting was on June 5, 1968. This was just two months after Martin Luther King was shot, three years after Malcolm X was shot, and five years after JFK and Medgar Evers were shot. Sirhan Sirhan shot Bobby Kennedy, the younger brother of the late President John Kennedy, in the ballroom of the Ambassador Hotel in Los Angeles, California. Bobby, the newly elected senator from New York, had just won the California Democratic primary to be nominated to run for the office of president of the United States. In less than five years, all these remarkable men were assassinated with guns, not in the dead of night (except Malcolm X) when no one could see, but smack-dab in front of all of us, in broad daylight—sometimes with the TV cameras rolling. All five men were husbands and fathers. Something was wrong in America, all right.

Two years later, at 12:24 p.m. on May 4, 1970, bullets flew again. Thirteen college students at Kent State, in Kent, Ohio, got in the way of bullets fired by the Ohio National Guard. Four of them got so far in the way that they died. Nine others were wounded. Two of those who died were at a student protest where several thousand students gathered because President Nixon had recently announced that he had directed the US armed forces in Vietnam to invade Cambodia, the country next door.

The other two students who died were just walking from one class to another. One was in the ROTC program at Kent State. Kent State is 191 miles northeast of Yellow Springs, Ohio.

In anticipation of this student demonstration, there were seventy-seven National Guardsmen present—Companies A and C of the 1/145th Infantry and Troop G of the 2/107th Armored Cavalry. Sergeant Myron Pryor began firing his .45 pistol at 12:24 p.m. Twenty-eight more of them took aim and fired their M-1 rifles at students. There was much confusion. There was noise. One guard member said he'd heard the order to shoot. Other guard members said they never heard an order. Some soldiers thought they heard a shot coming at them from the students. Others said they heard nothing but the shots fired by other soldiers.

There was a part-time student there that day. He was identified by other Kent State students. His name was Terry Norman. He was there to take pictures of the leaders of the protest. Students knew he was an informant for the campus police and for the Akron division of the FBI. Later in 1970, J. Edgar Hoover would say Norman never worked for the FBI. He would say this to a bunch of congressman in a public hearing on Capitol Hill. Oddly, Terry Norman would not agree with J. Edgar Hoover.

Norman was there that day taking pictures. He had a gas mask and was armed with a pistol. Three years later, an Indiana congressman would tell the governor of Ohio that he believed, based on what an Ohio State guardsman had told him, the soldiers were responding to a shot fired at them. The soldiers thought it was Norman who fired the shot.

In two years, in May of 1972, J. Eger Hoover died of a heart attack. Many people in Washington and around the world slept much better the day his death was announced. I was now twenty-three. I would graduate college in several weeks. I was in the "home stretch." Bill Gates was seventeen years old. While I was celebrating finishing college with another Stroh's beer, Bill Gates was busy wowing his teachers in high school. Soon he would go to Harvard and then drop out to form Microsoft and become a gazillionaire. Steve Jobs was six months older than Bill. He would attend Reed College in Oregon, only to also drop out, form Apple, and become a gazillionaire too.

Richard Nixon was fifty-nine years old. In two years, he would make history for actions unbecoming a president—or anyone else.

1964

As I said, I was a tavern boy at Ye Old Tavern right on Main Street (actually 228 Xenia Avenue) in downtown Yellow Springs. Ohio was one of those states that sold "up" and "down" beer. Down beer was 3.2 percent alcohol, and up beer was the real deal, 6 percent. At eighteen years old, you could buy and drink down beer, but you had to be twenty-one years old to drink up beer or to serve or sell either. There were four of us college students who worked there. Tim from New Orleans, a short little guy who looked like he was sixteen, was the only one of us who was actually twenty-one.

The Tavern was across the street from Furay's Hardware Store, the Yellow Gulch Saloon, the laundromat, and the Yellow Springs Bakery, which opened daily at midnight. Everyone went there to satisfy late-night pot-smoking munchies with their famous glazed donuts fresh from the oven. They melted in your mouth and were to-die-for.

In 1944, Mr. and Mrs. Furay, the owners of the hardware store, had a son named Richie who would grow up and play the electric guitar. He left Yellow Springs in 1964 and went to New York City to make his mark in the music industry. There, he met another unknown singer and guitar player named Stephen Stills. Together they would form the Buffalo Springfield Band with another unknown musician named Neil Young. Stephen Stills would later form Crosby, Stills & Nash, sometimes joined by Neil Young.

Richie had a long road to follow, and he made music with many more rock and roll giants along the way: giants like Neil Young, Jim Messina, and Kenny Loggins. Eventually he and some others including Jim Messina created POCO, the first but short-lived rock and roll/country band in the very late sixties and early seventies. Later on, Jim Messina would eventually team up with Kenny Loggins to form a very successful duo. Another musician in the group, Randy Meisner, left POCO and was asked to join a new band Glenn Frey and Don Henley were putting together called the Eagles. Now get this: when Randy Meisner left POCO, he was replaced by Tim Schmit. Years later, in 1977, Randy Meisner was on the move again and left the Eagles. He was replaced once again by that same Tim Schmit. The Eagles were having a Disney moment. "It's a small world after all": in the early days of rock and roll, on most days, rock and roll was a very small world.

In 1964, I was fifteen years old. Stephen Stills was nineteen. Richie Furay was twenty. Mick Jagger was twenty-one. Jimmy Hendrix was twenty-two. John Lennon was twenty-four.

Louis Armstrong was sixty-three years old. Soon he would sing the Broadway show tune "Hello, Dolly!" and put it on his new album. The show opened in January of 1964. It was a smash hit. Louis Armstrong's album *Hello, Dolly!* came out several months after the Broadway opening. His album became the number one album in the United States as reported by *Billboard* magazine in June of 1964.

Main Street was pretty much the only commercial street in Yellow Springs, Ohio. Good grief, you could drive through that town in less time than it took to sneeze. And yes, there really is a yellow spring. It's in Glen Helen, across the street from the college. I took a picture of it.

This picture hangs in my house. It's a black-and-white photo, so you can't really tell the spring is yellow.

I took a girl named Sarah on a walk in the Glen in the fall of 1968. This was not our first walk. But this time we kissed, and I touched her breasts. She had wonderful breasts to kiss and touch. She had on the kind of shirt that in the late sixties invited certain young men to come right on in and do just that. I knew she was going with a guy, but she let me kiss and fondle her anyway. We stopped going for walks together after that, but late one night in 1970, she knocked on the door of my dormitory room and asked to come in. She had had a fight with the new fellow she was then living with. She did not explain what the fight was about, and I did not ask. No history was given, none required. Now if you are going to sleep with another student on a college dormitory bed, you better be prepared—purposefully or accidently—to rub, touch, and nestle all areas of your body with the other person's. There's just no avoiding it.

Sarah's boyfriend was not a student. He was teaching a class at the college on combustion engine motors: cars and motorcycles. In fact, he was helping me fix my Harley. I had lent it to a friend who'd fallen off it while riding slowly in a field. The friend had left it on its side so long that all the oil drained out of it. This damaged the motor. My friend eventually got back on and began to ride it all over Yellow Springs. In almost no time, while he was stopped at one of the town's three traffic lights, the motor seized. It now needed new pistons and new rings. Currently housed in Len's classroom, the motor was in more pieces than a backyard swing set fresh out of the box. But it was OK. Len was a genius with motors.

"Can I stay with you?"

"Of course. Are you sure?" I asked her, knowing full well she was going with Len. I was unsure of what "staying here" meant. I was ill at ease, but I was excited.

We did make love. Life is often simple when you are twenty-one years old. That one night was all the universe had in mind for us. Sometimes it goes that way.

Strange Bedfellows

Let's back up for a minute. In 1962, I watched on TV as a US National Guard commander told the governor of Mississippi to step aside and let one of his state citizens enter a public state college he had been accepted to. All the students there were white. The young veteran attempting to enter the university was black. The governor was white. The National Guard was white, too. The 503rd Military Police Battalion and the US Border Patrol were sent. They were also white. The students rioted and mayhem ensued; hundreds were injured. A French journalist was shot dead. I was thirteen. I did not understand.

But with the help of five hundred federal marshals and Bobby Kennedy, the attorney general of the United States, James Meredith entered the University of Mississippi on October 1, 1962. This air force veteran, a member of the beat generation, lived in a dorm. To ensure he would get a good night's sleep, white students who lived above him took turns bouncing basketballs all night. In the cafeteria, if he sat down at a table with white students, they would all get up and sit somewhere else. Welcome to the University of Mississippi, James Meredith.

It took not one, but two decisions by the US Supreme Court even to get him to the front door—two decisions and a proclamation by the president of the United States that said anyone standing in James's way to this university had to move. The first court decision was in 1954: *Brown v. Board of Education* decreed that public schools had to be desegregated. The second overturned the conviction on his police record for "false voter registration." False voter registration convictions were one tool Mississippi and other southern states used to keep black people from participating in the American dream. False voter registration was a felony. Felons could not vote anywhere in America. Felons could not obtain public housing—or, in some states, be accepted into public colleges.

In 1963, I watched Governor George Wallace of Alabama block two black (accepted) students from Alabama attempt to register to attend another all-white state university.

"...I say segregation now, segregation tomorrow, segregation forever..." he had said recently in his inaugural speech.

He actually stood in the doorway so they could not enter the building. General Henry Graham asked him to move. He would not move so the general called up President Kennedy. President Kennedy federalized the general's troops.

"Sir, it is my sad duty to ask you to step aside under the orders of the President of the United States". He had five hundred National Guard troops with him. Governor Wallace spoke for a moment and then moved.

Soon Bob Dylan would immortalize the moment in his song: The Times They Are A Changing.

> .....'Come senators and congressmen
> Please heed the call
> Don't stand in the doorways
> Don't block up the halls.....'

Later that same year, Wallace decided to run for president of the United States. Shortly after he began his campaign, someone shot him, too—again in broad daylight, with the cameras rolling.

I was entering prep school when James Meredith graduated from the University of Mississippi. When James graduated from college, Michael Jordan, the basketball player, was five years old. James Meredith entered Columbia University and earned a law degree. No federal marshals were needed there.

James Meredith did not play basketball, but he paved the way for black people to vote in Mississippi. He also paved the way for Michael Jordan, who would play basketball for the University of North Carolina at Chapel Hill nineteen years later. As a freshman, Michael helped them win a national championship in 1982. With seventeen seconds left, he scored the winning basket that put North Carolina back in the lead.

They say politics makes strange bedfellows. James Meredith was to become the living proof of that. From 1989 to 1991, the very black James Meredith served the extremely white Senator Jesse Helms, the avowed segregationist from North Carolina, as his domestic adviser. The conservative Senator Helms had spent a lifetime obstructing civil rights, voting rights, integration of public schools, abortion, women's rights, and gay rights. He often said that the Civil Rights Bill of 1964 was perhaps the most dangerous piece of legislation Congress ever passed. Now, twenty-five years later in 1989 the first black to enroll at the University of Mississippi was working for him.

"Can you dig that?" Dick Caplan said, smiling. "I guess the times they really were changing".

In 1989, I was forty years old. Barack Obama was twenty-eight. In 1988, Barack entered Harvard Law School. In 1988, George W. Bush was forty-three years old. In April of that year, Bush purchased some shares of the Texas Rangers baseball team for $800,000 and became a general manager. In 1998, he sold his shares and made over $15 million.

In 2004, Garry Trudeau, the creator of the syndicated *Doonesbury* cartoon series, would give an interview to the *New York Times* magazine. He was asked if he had known George W. Bush when they had both been at Yale. Garry said he did know him and then told a story about the first interview George W. Bush ever gave to a big-city reporter. Bush's fraternity at Yale had been in the national news. They had been *branding* new recruits. The *New York Times* came to do the story. They interviewed W.

"And Bush described the branding as no worse than a cigarette burn" said Trudeau. "His first interview in the national media was in defense of torture." added Trudeau.

A California Bungalow

OUR HOUSE IN WALLINGFORD WAS built in 1918, by a builder who was born at the end of the American Civil War. Like me, he too was kind of a postwar baby. This baby's father, a builder in the late 1880s, was one of those lucky-to-be-alive fellows who came back from our Civil War. Six hundred thousand of them did not come back. In 1918, right there on Long Hill Road, in Wallingford, Connecticut the son of the lucky-to-be-alive builder built a two-bedroom, one-bath California bungalow. In the years to come, they would add a garage with two bedrooms and another bath above it.

In 1968, that same Civil War veteran's grandson, John, running that same construction company, remodeled that same house for my father. And in 1983, John, then already in his late sixties, and I, in my mid-thirties, would experience a short future together. It was right before his construction company, which had survived over one hundred years, gave up on the future and became part of Wallingford's past.

In 1939, when my dad bought the California bungalow, he was thirty-five years old. The house was twenty-one years old. Tom Caplan was about to get married to that hot-ticket salesgirl from New Haven, Connecticut, with the black hair, full figure, and smile that caused grown men to act like teenage boys.

In 1918, when our future house was being built, my dad was fourteen years old, driving a horse and buggy to pick up fresh fruit and vegetables. While bullets, bombs, and poison gas were all over Europe, he was a freshman in high school, helping his mother run a small grocery and meat shop. I have a picture of him sitting on the front steps of his high school in his football uniform. The year was 1921; it said so on the ball. He was seventeen years old. This old high school building was just blocks from the center of Wallingford. Now, like the entire class of 1921, it is long gone.

In 1919, my dad wasn't driving a horse and buggy anymore. He was driving an old Model-T Ford truck. You had to know how to drive it, but you didn't need a driver's license. In Connecticut, you did not have to have one until 1921. In the mid-twenties, his younger brother Itzie broke his arm trying to start that old Model-T. At the front of the car, below the radiator, was the crank to start the motor.

Tom ran the store with his mother, but in the fall, she would make sure he had time to play football on the high school team. He had to. He was the quarterback.

My dad had on shoulder pads in the picture. In 1921, your own shoulders were mostly your shoulder pads. The helmet was leather. There was no face mask. No one knew about repeated head trauma yet. Speaking of pictures, forty-three years later, someone hung a picture of me in my high school football uniform in the Caplan's Supermarket office. My helmet was made of sturdy plastic, and it had a face guard. It looked considerably safer than my father's helmet, but in reality, it would not protect my head from repeated head trauma, either.

Tom was the middle of three boys born to Samuel and Dora. Remember, I told you my father's parents were Jewish Russian immigrants whose marriage was arranged. Now my dad helped his mother run the little grocery and meat market. He played football, too. The oldest boy and the youngest boy were not interested in the little store. When my dad graduated from high school, he went into business with his mother.

So where was his father? Ugh. Listen, neither my sisters nor I can remember even *one* story our own father told us about his dad. And our paternal grandfather died before the oldest of us was even six years old. We don't know the details of our grandfather, Sam Caplan's life here in America, but we do know that at a very young age, this second-born son of his, Thomas, and his wife Dora, Thomas's Russian-born mother, began a journey together to seek and attain the American dream.

In 1918, while our future house at 88 Long Hill Road was being built, Marian Puklin—my maternal grandmother—was about to give birth to her first child, a baby girl she and her husband would name Evelyn. She was a lucky little baby, for a moment. She was born into a very wealthy family.

During the late twenties, while my dad and his mother were busy finding economic success here in America, my ten-year-old mother's family was losing her paternal grandfather's second fortune. It took decades for Morris Puklin, Evelyn's grandfather, to go from rags to riches. In 1929, however, the reverse process took less time than cooking an egg over easy. The only one close to my mom's family who still had a buck in his pocket was the chauffeur, who did not believe in banks or stock markets. He kept his money in a box buried under the back porch, where the garden tools were stored.

Living in the Moment

IN 1949, I WAS BRAND-NEW. My sisters tell me I was interested mainly in was my mother's breasts. I was living in the moment. Years later, I would receive that advice again: to live in the moment. And as far as breasts go, I have never needed anyone to tell me to maintain my interest in them.

Unless it was raining, my sisters and I walked almost a half mile to Simpson Elementary School every day. We walked home for lunch, back to school for the afternoon session, and then home again at 3:00 p.m. Lucky for me, the school had a playground. Otherwise, I am not sure I would have had any use for it. Older people attempted to civilize me during the fifties. Some employed wisdom that I still draw on. Others used shame and doubt that unfortunately still find their ways into my life. None of them had more than moderate success.

Stuff I learned in the fifties that was important to me: how to ride a bike, swing a bat, light a campfire, catch a baseball, shoot a rifle, throw a football, whittle with a knife, dribble a basketball, fake one way and drive to the basket another, use a hatchet, swim, pretend to be shot in war and fall down dead, water ski, snow ski, dive into a pool, pack a grocery bag, and stock a shelf. Stuff that was important to other people: how to dress myself, print letters and words, read, share, tie shoelaces (wasn't that a bitch!), dance, buckle a belt, shake hands, play checkers, write thank-you notes, add, subtract, divide, multiply, blow my nose, read Hebrew, use some good manners, mow a lawn, be nice to my sisters, shovel snow, and wash cars.

"Danger, Will Robinson, danger!" said the TV.

IN THE EARLY SIXTIES, RIGHT around the season when the Connecticut autumn evenings sneak right up on you and all of a sudden it's almost dark, my buddy Allen and I were walking up Center Street from his house on Whittlesey Avenue to my house up on Long Hill Road, a good mile and a half. We were both eleven years old. Right before the turn onto Long Hill Road, a car pulled over and three young hoods got out and stood in front of us, making us stop on the sidewalk.

"Hey, Lenny, let's give these nice boys a ride home," said the tallest one, pointing his finger at us and laughing. His name was Vinnie, we'd learn. He was smoking a cigarette. His cigarette pack was rolled up under the right sleeve of his dirty white T-shirt, up by his shoulder. That shirt was ready for a Tide commercial. The three of them smelled like beer.

"Sure thing, Vinnie," said the shorter one. "We can give them a real sweet ride." Vinnie was the leader, all right. The other two now stood behind him on the sidewalk. He told us to get into their car, a 1955 Chevy. We said no, and the other two started pushing Allen. They asked, "What's da matter boys, don't you like our car?"

The next moment, an adult stopped his car right in the middle of the road and told those boys to be on their way or he would help them get there; he could see they were up to no good. One of them said something smart, and the guy put his car in park and started to get out, right in the middle of the road. The punks got in their car and left without saying another word. To show how tough they were, they peeled out, burning some rubber. He asked us where we lived and drove us home.

I met that man again many years later, at my insurance agent's annual holiday party in Wallingford. The man knew who I was and refreshed my memory. We shook hands. I thanked him, and I introduced him to Karen, my wife. I hadn't thought about that moment in many years.

Later at the party, I thought about that moment some more and began to fully realize the significance of his actions that night. I decided I needed to go thank him again. I went back to find him. "I just had to shake hands with you one more time," I said. "I hope you don't mind."

The Land

THE LAND MY DAD BOUGHT in the center of town, the same land that would come to dominate my life, sat but a mile away from our house on Long Hill Road. One of the buildings on the land was a big old barn. Actually, there were several barns. This one was red. In 1959, the paint was peeling because it was over a hundred years old.

I was ten years old and pretty much unaware of anything outside of my small town. Heck, I wasn't even fully aware of most things inside my small town. For instance, I did not know that Lyman Hall, a signer of the Declaration of Independence, was born here and has a monument dedicated to him in the 340-year-old cemetery down-town. You would not know there was a cemetery there because there is a high cement wall around it. That's right, a thick cement wall. Not a sweet wrought-iron fence that would show off the look of this historic landmark.

Lyman Hall signed the Declaration of Independence in 1776. In 1884, one E. E. Hall ran a livery stable from this same barn with the peeling red paint. Perhaps he was a cousin of Mr. Lyman Hall. The Halls were one of the founding families of Wallingford. One Hall begat another in 1670, and then there was more begetting, and voilà—in 1776 we have a Lyman Hall, followed by an E. E. Hall in 1884. There are twenty-three Halls listed in the white pages of the 2012 Wallingford telephone book.

The old red paint on the barn was so flaky that from a distance, it looked like a Jackson Pollock painting. In 1955, Jackson Pollock was forty-three years old. I was six. At the age of twenty-one, during the early 1930s, Mr. Pollock moved to New York City from his home in Wyoming. He was to become a famous painter of modern art. When I was fourteen years old, I went with my eighth grade class on a field trip to NYC. It was amazing. We visited the Statue of Liberty and the Museum of Modern Art. There I saw his work displayed as an example of abstract expressionism.

"What the heck is that?" I asked my buddy Billy.

"I'm not sure," said Billy O'Dell. He was standing next to me. We'd also sat next to each other on the bus ride to New York. He did not have a clue. "Where's the picture?"

"Billy, I think I could do that art," I said, surprised at myself.

Jackson Pollock would become famous for something else. He would be known for being the life of the party. But because he drank so much gin, many people experienced him as the death of the party as well.

On August 11, 1956, while driving on Long Island just a mile from his new home, Jackson Pollock would make a bad decision concerning several bottles of gin and an automobile he was driving. On this day, at the age of 44, the Jackson Pollock show would end forever on Heartbreak Earth. Andy Warhol was 28 years old. Barbara Streisand was 14 years old. My mother was 38 years old. In 1956, New York City was 334 years old. No one really knows how old "art" is.

Everyone's House Shook

My dad's immigrant parents lived in a two-family house right on the corner of Church and North Colony Streets here in Wallingford. The little store was on the first floor, and the family lived upstairs. This corner was at the bottom of a hill. The upper highway (soon to called North and South Main Streets) was where the original settlers of Wallingford had carved out forty-two rectangular plots of six acres each to be settled by a family.

About two hundred years later, housing and commerce settled where North and South Main was split by Center Street, the real center of the town. The farms were now relocated farther from the town center and increased in size well beyond the six-acre plots. Soon the original plots were sold to become housing for this growing community. Center Street would have all the businesses. Other streets off North and South Main would emerge with two and three family housing. The further down the hill one went, the cheaper the housing became. In the nineteenth and early twentieth centuries, immigrants who spoke Hungarian, Russian, German, Yiddish, Italian, Portuguese, Polish, and other European languages lived in those multi-family houses.

As a boy, my father went sledding with his brothers and his friends on one of those streets that went down the hill. When it snowed, the police would close it so the children could sled there.

At the bottom of the hill were the train tracks. They ran parallel. South of Wallingford, in New Haven, the railroad tracks split. One set followed the coast northeast through Providence and Boston to Maine. The other branch traveled due north through Wallingford, Hartford, Springfield, and points north all the way to Canada. In those days, all the houses within two or three blocks of the tracks shook every time a train came by. In 1910, up and down North and South Colony Streets, all the houses shook including my dad's

Thirty years later, if you were an independent supermarket and you could store or sell enough cases to make it worth their while, big companies from all over the United States sold their products directly to you. They dropped off railroad cars in the railroad yards of small towns and big cities—wherever the big supermarkets were. Then they sent the key to the locked boxcars to the owner of the supermarket. My dad was one of those owners. He sent men down to the yard in big trucks to empty those boxcars and bring the goods back to the barns on the land he'd bought so he could buy in bulk and get better pricing. At one point, he had three old barns full of Scott's toilet paper, Bounty paper towels, Tide detergent, Windex glass cleaner, SOS pads, and Dial soap.

Toward the end of each summer, Tom would go out to Minnesota to buy thousands of pounds of Land o' Lakes butter, Land o' Lakes American cheese, Butterball turkeys, and specialty cheeses. He would buy them for the holidays and then bring them back with him on the train. The refrigerated boxcars would go right to New Haven Cold Storage on Long Wharf in New Haven, Connecticut. Everything he bought would be gone by New Year's. He would buy thousands of turkeys. For many years, all the factories in Wallingford gave their employees turkeys for Thanksgiving or Christmas. And all the factories in Wallingford bought their turkeys from Tom. He would buy direct before many of us knew what direct meant.

Caplan's Supermarket

SAMUEL AND DORA STARTED THEIR little store around 1897. But by 1923, Dora and her son Tom were partners. He was nineteen years old. In 1930, they did $59,861.51 in sales for the entire year. By the early fifties, Tom and his brother Itzie would do that in one month. In 1960, it took them less than a week and a half.

Tom knew everyone. Everyone knew Tom. He was always engaged with children. He was earnest, responsive, honest, handsome, sincere, and authentic. He was in demand. He needed to be caught up on someone's daughter's newborn, or a son trying to get into West Point. Could he help? Someone was down on her luck. Could she charge some groceries? Did he know that so-and-so died, or so-and-so was accepted into college? A new European arrival from the old country needed a job, or a child wanted to hold Tom's hand and ask if he had any candy. As I said, everyone needed to talk to him. It really was his town.

In Wallingford, from the twenties to the seventies, there was only one local place to buy quality meats: Caplan's Supermarket. People came from all over Wallingford. People also came from the surrounding towns: Cheshire, Hamden, Meriden, Durham, Middlefield, Northford, and North Haven. It was a supermarket, but they came for the meats. They lined up in front of the fifty foot meat counter ten deep.

On Thursdays and Fridays in the late fifties and early sixties, if you had a shopping cart—and in spite of the three women working at the deli counter and the six men behind the meat counter—it was going to take you some time to go down the extra-wide, eighty-foot-long first aisle. It was Wallingford's version of Times Square. And there were more butchers in back who came out to serve customers when needed.

When it really got busy, my dad or my uncle would go to the counter. There were no boys behind that meat counter then; just men who knew cuts of meat and how to *kibitz* (Yiddish for someone who watches the action and makes comments). Customers were not simply waited on—they were engaged, educated, and entertained while they purchased their meats.

The butchers waited on newlyweds who did not know what they wanted, how much of it they needed, or what to do with it when they got it; they waited on older housewives who knew exactly what they wanted and needed no advice on preparation or cooking. The women chatted with their friends while they waited. They caught up on news, children, employment, schools, marriages, deaths, or births. No one was in a hurry except the men behind the meat counter. Odd as it may sound today, many people were actually enjoying themselves. At the meat counter, being waited on, they were king or queen. The counter staff treated everyone as if they were royalty, and the customers loved it.

The butchers were not just selling meat; they were selling a delicious meal. It wasn't a sale; it was a dance with a man wearing a long white coat and a white apron tied over it. These men were Polish, French Canadian, Russian, Italian, or Hungarian, and all could put a smile on most any face. Oh, the accents! They were older and could advise on all aspects of meat preparation: cooking temperatures, special cuts, bone-in or boneless. They could explain the differences between porterhouse, sirloin, skirt, or chuck steaks and tell you how best to cook pot roasts, oven roasts, rib roasts, and crown roasts. They knew how to butterfly a leg of lamb, cut veal for cutlets, barbecue, make a meat loaf, cut and saw pork chops and prepare deer meat. The older ones could slaughter and butcher cattle, chickens, ducks, rabbits, geese, fish, deer, pigs, or lamb.

Steve, the head butcher, was Polish. He created a recipe for Italian sausage so good it required him to make several hundred pounds twice each week. Steve himself mixed fennel, salt, pepper, and several secret ingredients right into the boned, trimmed, and cubed pork butts. Then it was ground and eventually fed into another grinder with long tube where the meat came out. We poured water on the tube to keep it wet and slippery and slid animal intestines over the end so the mixture came out enclosed in a clear, balloon-like casing.

Back then, the beef, pork, and lamb all came to the store "on the hoof." It had to be broken down. Now it comes in boxes already broken down into steaks, roasts, legs of lambs, and such.

Phil was young in the fifties, right out of high school. He worked in the meat room. He was over six feet tall and weighed just a bit over 260 pounds. He had arms of steel. He could receive a 160-pound side of beef, raise it over his head, and hook it on a receiving roller hanging from the black iron rail suspended from the ceiling just inside the door. A foot or so down the rail, the side of beef was weighed. Farther down, the rail went into the cooler and then to a panel above the cooler door which split open after taking a sharp right into the cooler; once inside the cooler, the rails split off into three sections: one for beef, one for pork, and one for lamb. It was like a railroad yard upside down.

The cooler door was a Jamison, the Cadillac of cooler doors. It was ten inches thick and so heavy it had three hinges that were each twelve inches long.

In the early sixties, I used to put fresh sawdust on the hardwood floor each night, after sweeping up the previous day's sawdust and the blood and droppings it had absorbed. All the machines were taken apart each night to be washed and wiped down. All the wooden butcher blocks were scraped and dry-scrubbed with sawdust after most every use. They were almost two feet thick and weighed hundreds of pounds. We used a wire brush and then wiped them clean. No acrylic chopping blocks yet. Every Saturday afternoon, as far back as I can remember, the entire meat room was taken apart and steam-cleaned.

The bag boys took your groceries out to your car. They carried them out or put them in the cart and pushed the cart right to your car. Either way, you did not touch them until you got home. If you wanted, Caplan's would deliver your groceries. In the early sixties, it cost thirty-five cents to have them delivered. You could even call your order in. It was mostly the elderly who did so. They had been shopping at Caplan's for decades. There was no charge for the shopping.

The part-timers who stocked the shelves and worked on the deli and meat counters or packaged produce in the morning were hardworking guys who had full-time jobs in the factories. They would work for Tom until two o'clock and then go to lunch. They would arrive at the factories at three, work until eleven at night, go home and get some sleep, and get to Caplan's by eight or nine the following morning.

At two thirty in the afternoon, the women who had rung the registers all morning left. They had houses to clean, children coming home from school, suppers to prepare, and clothes to wash. They were replaced by high school girls. High school boys would stock shelves, clean the meat room, package produce, bag groceries, and carry them out to the cars. They would work until six on Mondays, Tuesdays, Wednesdays, and Saturdays. Thursdays and Fridays, some stayed until nine o'clock. All the part-time employees were supervised by department managers or full-time workers.

We were closed on Sundays. Everything was closed on Sundays. Sunday was God's day. Remember that God whom the beings of *incorrigible behavior and armed conflict* refused to share? Well, toward the end of the twentieth century, that God now had to share his day, Sunday, with another God—the money God: Walmart, malls, liquor stores, car dealers, pawn shops and supermarkets.

In the basement of *the Building* is an old metal accounting rack that stored the unpaid charge accounts. During the thirties, many families could not pay for groceries. Most of these families were great customers in the twenties. In the thirties, they were still good customers; they just did not have much money. Some paid a little each week.

Our next-door neighbor on Long Hill Road told me a story one day in the late fifties. We were in her backyard. Her husband, Fred, had been retired ever since I could remember. On the night before Halloween, my neighborhood buddy Skipper and I would ring their doorbell and then go hide across the street on the golf course. "You ring this doorbell one more time, Dicky Caplan, and I will tell your father!" Fred would shout into the night from his front door.

"After World War Two started, there were some food items no one could get," his wife told me. "Your dad would put the butter or the sugar on the bottom of the bag so no one could see them if they looked inside the truck at all the groceries being delivered. When the groceries came here, I would find these presents on the bottom of bag. Your dad told me not to say anything. I never told a soul." She was dead serious.

"Tom admired his mother to bits. She taught him well. They had a strong bond" said Claire, my dad's secretary.

Inside the home that Tom bought the family on North Main Street, ill and close to death, Dora made Tom promise to take care of his brothers and his father no matter what. It was Christmas Eve, 1943.

"Family was everything to Dora," said Claire. "To save her own brothers, she had left her parents in Russia to marry someone she did not even know and then one by one bring them here to America."

I have wondered for years what my dad's mom thought about all her boys, about her life, about her husband, about her Tommy. Whom did her Tommy remind her of?

On the Caplan side of my family, my father and his brothers were the first generation who married for love; all marriages before them were arranged by matchmakers. My sisters and I were the second generation.

"Can you dig it?" I said to my new college best friend, Chris.

"Far out," said Chris. He really meant it.

Some Things Are Just Harder Than Others

IN THE LATE FIFTIES, MANY people had forgotten that just a short forty-five years earlier, almost everyone traveled by horse and buggy. If you did not remember, you might wonder what the heck this flaky old barn was doing right in the center of our New England town. In the fifties, unless they lived on a ranch, most young people certainly could not remember having horses everywhere. We boomers grew up with cars, TVs, stereos, snap jacks, Hula Hoops, Slinkys, the Good Humor ice cream truck, *MAD* magazines, record albums, jet airplanes, atomic bombs, and rock and roll. Unless you lived in certain parts of the country or at a racetrack, the presence of lots of horses was reserved for television, parades, and the circus.

In my father's lifetime, travel had evolved from horse and buggies to spaceships. At the age of thirteen, in 1917, he regularly drove a horse and buggy to pick up fresh fruit and vegetables. A few years later, he drove a used Model-T Ford truck, then cars: Packards, Chevys, and finally Oldsmobiles. Later in life, he could have driven Cadillacs or even BMWs or Audis, but he was not that kind of man.

In 1961, he watched Alan Shepard blast off into space on the first manned space flight. It lasted fifteen minutes. Seven years later, on July 20, 1968—just months after Martin Luther King and Bobby Kennedy were assassinated—he watched astronauts land on the moon. A moment later, he watched Neil Armstrong become the first man to walk there. In the late sixties, human beings figured out how to land on the moon and fly back to earth, but not how to stop killing earthlings they had never met. For human beings, I guess, some things are just harder than others.

"He started with horses, all right, and ended with spaceships. Can you dig it?" I told everybody in 1969.

"Far out!" they said right back to me.

The columns that supported the old red barn on our land had bite marks in them. Long ago, horses in stalls used to bite them so regularly that most of the columns had old rusted mesh wire nailed to them to protect them from all the chewing. As a young boy, I watched a man cut the beams holding the old barn up.

"What are we going to do to the barn?" I asked.

"We are going to take it down," the man said in his thick French Canadian accent. The man cutting the beams was born in Canada. Some beams were cut through. Some beams were only cut partially. When he was through cutting, he connected chains to those beams and attached them to a dump truck parked right outside. The dump truck was owned by my father.

"Where is everyone?" I asked.

"Who"? The man had a puzzled look, as if he did not understand the question.

"You know, everyone who's going to help us take down the barn," I said. "We'll need a lot of men."

"We are going to take it down ourselves," he said calmly. My dad, knowing his work in the lumber camps, had asked him to take the barn down before it fell down on its own. The gray-haired man told me to move out of the way. Then he got into the truck, started it up, and drove forward. The chains tightened and rose up off the ground.

The beams and supporting columns began to moan and then to voice consecutive and consistent discontent by splitting in two—but not all at once. They split in order, like when the waiter brings a meal: first the drink, then some bread, then the salad or soup or appetizer, then the main course, then some coffee, and finally dessert.

In a moment, the barn was going to prove Newton's laws of gravity. First, the roof fell in onto the second-floor loft; then the second floor fell straight down to the ground floor. The back of the barn collapsed onto the already fallen roof, the front fell in on that, and finally both sides of the barn fell flat. It was magic. The entire building had, in a matter of seconds, caved on itself like a house of cards. It fell about as fast as the economy did in the fall of 1929 and again in the fall of 2008.

It wasn't really magic. The Frenchman was not a magician. He was not an engineer, either. In fact, he had never taken a building down before. He couldn't operate a slide rule. He'd never learned algebra, because he'd never gone to high school. He didn't know who Newton was. But he certainly knew how to make large things fall down where he wanted them to fall. Long ago, as a young man, he'd lived in Maine and worked in the logging camps. He regularly brought down monstrous trees exactly where the camp boss had instructed him to. His name was Fred LaBelle. Everyone called him Freddy.

The barn said, "Ka-boom!" and down it came.

In 1959, when the barn came down, I was still ten years old. Sam Huff, number 70, the great center linebacker for the New York Giants, was twenty-five. And the tallest athlete in the world, the seven-foot-one-inch Wilt Chamberlain, was twenty-three years old. He was graduating from college. The year 1959 was his first in the NBA. In 1959, Michael Jordan was not yet born. Wilt would go on to have a great rivalry with the shorter but incredibly talented Bill Russell of the Boston Celtics. Wilt died in 1999, at the age of sixty-three. In 1999, Michael Jordan was thirty-six years old. At the time, Michael, like Wilt, was all through with basketball. Sixteen years later, in 2015, Sam Huff was eighty years of age and still kicking.

The Chain Stores Are Coming! The Chain Stores Are Coming!

In the late fifties, manufacturing companies stopped selling direct to the men who owned independent supermarkets in America. No more dropping off locked railroad cars and mailing the owner the key. Now independent supermarkets had to buy from wholesale companies with large warehouses right here in Connecticut and every other state. Instead of having forty or fifty providers of goods, now you could simply call one provider.

All the dry goods you bought were delivered to your back door; some companies sold you frozen, meat, deli, and produce, too. Of course, they charged a fee for their services. It sounded good on paper. In reality, it was the beginning of the end for the independent single-supermarket owner. But it had been a good thirty-year run. Soon, these independent supermarkets would be the kind of store that an individual could no longer own *one* of. Eventually, one would need at least ten or twenty stores to operate competitively in the grocery business. Owning one or two hardware stores, drugstores, shoe stores, furniture stores, *anything* stores would soon not be viable. The chains were coming—the chains and the big-box stores. It would not be a slaughter. It would be a slow death that would take over thirty years. Corporate America was on the move. The rich were on the move.

Sticks and Stones

THE BLAIR ACADEMY PREPARATORY SCHOOL was set up on a hill overlooking a little village in a western New Jersey still surrounded by forests, meadows, and rolling hills. Prep schools were usually located in quaint old New England towns. If the prep school was located outside of New England, then the town hosting it was mandated to *look* like it belonged in New England. In the fall of 1963, I left Wallingford to attend this out-of-region "just like New England" prep school.

If you attended a prep school, then you know that all prep schools have a building called Memorial Hall, which is always built out of stone or red brick with big cathedral windows. This building is the chapel for the school, but it has many uses. All Memorial Halls are required to have a clock tower. These clock towers have chimes or bells so even students who are faraway or blind still know when it's time to change classes, go to lunch, or attend chapel.

In the sixties, the young people living in the town where the private school was located were called "townies" by the students. The young people who lived in the town where the prep school was located called the young boys who attended them "preppies." These two groups did not care much for one another. Much of that is still true.

Names have always been used to be insulting; they still are. For instance, white men in the South used to enjoy calling black men "niggers." They called them that when they were slaves. They still called them that after they were freed. Even though they were freed in the 1860s, a hundred years later black people in the South did not really possess any of the rights they had officially been granted. White people had hidden them in plain sight. If you were black and lived in the South, you could look at these rights, but not touch them or have them. When called niggers, they were not allowed to object. If they did, eventually they would be caught, tarred and feathered, whipped, or sometimes hanged. If you were someone who did these awful deeds, you need not worry about the police or the law; you just needed some rope and a big old tree. Often the police participated, too. Odd as it may sound, these white people who hanged black people liked to think of themselves as religious. Sometimes they lit ten-foot wooden crosses on fire.

I played football, tennis, and basketball, and I lettered in several sports. I was the News and then the Managing editor of the school paper, *The Blair Breeze.* I was in a service club called the Blue and White Key. Blue and White Key members gave campus tours to perspective students and their families or helped the wife of the headmaster get the weekly tea prepared—stuff like that. While I won the religion prize, I learned the meaning of the word "kike." I had some best friends. I knew some boys who hated me. When time allowed, I went to classes and managed to graduate with a school ring, a catalog of useful insults, a school blazer, a newfound love of writing, the possibility of a girlfriend, a letter of acceptance to Antioch College, significant lust for the football coach's wife, and a real dislike for the headmaster. The guy walked around as if he was God's gift to the world, just like the headmaster at the end of the movie *Scent of a Woman.* Those two could have been brothers.

In the spring of 1967, I was eighteen years old, a senior soon to graduate. As previously explained, I was now the Managing editor of the *Blair Breeze*. The June 1967 edition was my last paper. In case I had any thoughts of myself as a bright young lad, the school had recently sent me my class ranking: forty-fifth out of a class of seventy-eight boys. While I was not the brightest lamp in the room, I did know right from wrong. My father showed me.

On April 7, 1967, I watched three seniors stone a squirrel to death for fun. I wrote an editorial condemning these seniors. I did not reveal their names. Apparently the administration had no problem with the stoning; they were in cardiac arrest for a different reason. The alumni read the last paper of the year. It lists where all the seniors were going to college; apparently alumni liked to see how much smarter they were than the current graduates.

Freedom of the press was about to take a hit; I was about to 'take one for the the team', I was told. The faculty adviser enlisted the other student editors to ask me to withdraw the editorial. When that did not work, the faculty adviser asked me himself. Alumni could not read about this incident. Blair boys just did not behave like this. Then there was no more asking: there was telling. That was left to the headmaster. I can't tell you exactly what he said, but I can tell you it was in perfect English. The fact that I could not understand him was apparently more my problem than his. The editorial would not be printed. Graduation would not be tarnished.

In the years to come, I would learn I had a real knack for annoying people in authority.

A Fool's Errand

THE FIFTIES WERE VERY GOOD for small towns in America. But in less than ten years, across the country, these towns would be under attack by forces known as "progress." This progress came in two new building designs. No one knew it at first, but eventually we all realized that these two new building designs would be responsible for the end of Main Street almost everywhere in America.

One design was a collection of stores of various sizes built under one mother of a roof, most often at least two floors high. The structure included a big regional department store and was surrounded by parking lots big enough to fit small countries. The defining feature was that when you left one store to go to another, you were still out of the weather. They all had food courts, where many people were on their journeys to obesity, diabetes, and heart disease. People lined up for this path to an early death as if they were going to a new *Star Wars* movie. Small-town Main Street shopkeepers called the people who shopped in these malls 'maulers,' not because they shopped in malls, but because they tore the heart right out of downtowns all across America.

The other new building type was a single structure so large that some people thought they were new NFL football stadiums. They called this structure "the big-box store." It was initially hard to believe it was just one store. Even with roller skates on, one would need hours to navigate around it.

These new corporate retail stores were designed to employ hundreds of people who were paid so poorly that they never had a chance of owning a home, receiving proper health care, sending their children to college, having paid sick days, or paid vacations. They couldn't retire when they were sixty-five. What did they get? They got a 10 percent discount if they shopped in the store where they worked, owned by the same people who had offered them such a secure path to long-term poverty. America flocked to these new stores so fast and so often that by the late seventies you could set up ten pins on the main streets of every small and not-so-small town where, on the outskirts, "progress" had been built.

The people who owned the stores in the old downtowns of small-town America didn't know it, but they were done. They went to work each morning, but they were on a fool's errand. The busy downtowns of the eighteenth, nineteen, and early twentieth centuries—where citizens bought clothes, shoes, wedding gowns, food, and fuel; where they got haircuts, visited banks, went to the movies, ate ice cream, bought furniture, candy, sporting goods, bicycles, cameras, paints, building materials, jewelry, fabric, auto supplies and auto repairs, liquor, TVs, appliances, visited department stores, and so on—had been replaced. Their time was over, finished, kaput, ended, completed, all gone, done. It would take a little time for this progress to drive the last nail into their coffins, but twenty years later, all that was left in many downtowns were banks and insurance agencies, attorney's offices, real estate companies, restaurants, second-hand stores, ice cream parlors, flower shops, and a dozen hairdressers.

To add insult to injury, as more and more of these stores closed during the late seventies and eighties, small towns began fixing up their town centers, putting in new landscapes, brick sidewalks, new lights that looked like old-fashioned gaslights, and generally making their little downtown commercial areas look as they did in the eighteenth, nineteenth, and early twentieth centuries when real commerce actually took place there. They did it right here in my town. They blocked off the road for an entire summer and part of a fall while they performed all the renovations. It looked great when they finished. They put all the electric and telephone wires underground. They put down some red bricks for part of the sidewalks. You could even buy a brick and put your name or your parents' names on it! They planted fast-growing trees. The new lighting, in fact, looked like old gaslights. It was fabulous, all right, but the real commerce of an earlier time never returned. Empty storefronts popped up where in the past no vacancies existed long. Even cheap rent is expensive if customers do not come to your store.

Like many other stores, Caplan's Market closed begrudgingly. It was painful for me to say the least, but progress was calling out to all of us to reinvent ourselves, our buildings, our downtowns; to be imaginative, to work together to get it right.

Yellow Springs, Ohio

REGARDING MY BEHAVIOR AT ANTIOCH College between the fall of 1967 and the spring of 1972, let me say this right off the bat: I can probably no longer run for president of the United States. Actually, I'm sure. In fact, I know lots of people who cannot run for president. Too many people saw us roll, smoke, inhale, sniff, or swallow something—often, and with gusto.

I think of those days as an experiment. Whoever was in charge of the experiment was not from Heartbreak Earth. Antioch College was an unusual school. It was more like Summerhill for the college crowd.

Summerhill is a progressive private school—elementary to high school—in England. They believe that if left alone to work at their own pace, children and teenagers learn faster; <u>doing</u> was as important as listening. The subject or task is the means to an end, instead of an assignment. Often older students taught/advised younger students. There are no courses, no lesson plans. For example, children who wanted to learn about airplanes were encouraged to study airplanes. Having learned all they could from looking at pictures and perhaps wanting to know how something so heavy stayed up in the air, they were encouraged to learn how to read as teachers or older students offered them books which had the answers to their questions. Learning was self-motivated. It would become a constant experiment in seeking answers.

During the 1960's, much of ones education at Antioch College was self-designed or self-directed. If you wanted to learn psychology via English literature, one could. Of course one would eventually find English Literature professors limited in their ability to convey psychological theories or processes or what to say to help someone who was struggling with a psychological problem. Eventually, if you really wanted to learn about psychology, one might take psychology courses. It was designed to be a blended education to say the least. Certain courses at Antioch did have the traditional ingredients of what might be called normal college courses, but many were like a ride on a spaceship. Many of us perceived that there was no captain at the helm.

Of course, they designed it so you were the captain. You were the crew. Often you were the spaceship, too!

Your Number

ON DECEMBER 1, 1969, IT could be said that many a young man's number was up in America. The number depended on your birth date and a drawing held in Washington, DC. All the dates of the year were drawn one at a time out of a big bucket. They called it "the draft." If getting a chill is from a draft then this was a good name for it. In spite of a climate so hot that the sweat poured off of you, many men got so chilled from this draft that they never felt another thing again. We still have lotteries now, but if your number is called nowadays, you probably won a ton of money.

In those days, if America called your number, you would have to report to the army draft center to get a very short haircut and be yelled at by people you had never met for reasons that were never made clear. They seemed to believe you were currently less than human. Then they trained you to be killing machines. Once you were fixed, then you were sent halfway around the world to kill yellow men in a war in jungles in Southeast Asia.

In 1969, all young men born between 1944 and 1951 got a draft number and a draft card. It was free. After you filled out the form to register for a selective service number, the government mailed you your draft card when you turned eighteen years old. You were to carry your draft card in your wallet wherever you went. It was a law. I had one. Some young men who objected to this draft burned their draft card.

Before this lottery drawing, the United States was giving anyone who went to college or had a wife a deferment. The poor, who could not afford college, any unmarried men and young men who choose not to go to college were drafted. Then they'd be sent off to save the people of Vietnam from other people of Vietnam. Many died. Many in America did not think this draft business was fair, so politicians came up with the lottery. Americans used to be big on fairness. We are sometimes still big on fairness, but now you have to look hard for it. Now we are mostly big on money; mostly big money. We are big on quarterly earnings; we are really, really big on productivity and profit and loss stuff—mostly the profit.

As I said, this draft was only for young men. Women did not qualify for dying on the battlefield. Formally training them for battlefield duty would come in 2013.

So in 1969 they drew every date of the year out of a bucket. The ones they drew early had low numbers, and the ones they drew later had high numbers. You've probably already figured out it was good to have a high number. This lottery you actually won by losing. If the Pentagon did not call your number early, YOU WON!

Richard Caplan was born on April 9. His draft number was 219. He was a big-time winner. Like his father before him, but for different reasons, he would not go to war. In 1970, they stopped calling potential draftees at number 195. In future years, they wouldn't make it that far up the list. Had I been born on April 11, my number would have been 14. The birth date for number 195 was September 24. Know anyone born on October 24? His number was 196.

As I said, the reason there was a draft was that in the mid-sixties, thousands of boys came home from the war with only one leg or one arm or no legs at all. Their body parts were being regularly blown off them in booby traps and battles to discourage other young men from coming to the fight.

It worked, and soon many young men in America decided on Plan B. Plan A was to join the military. Plan B was anything else. For many young men who were to be drafted, Canada was Plan B. In the years to come, so many American citizens thought the Vietnam War was a poor decision by our government that the young men who moved to Canada were forgiven and invited to come home as citizens again, not as "draft dodgers" who would be put in prison.

The TV and newspaper industry in the United States covered this war. They showed it on TV every night. They published stories about it in the newspapers almost every day. Journalism was different in those days. They showed and wrote about war and injury and death as it actually happened, not as it was portrayed in the movies—no John Wayne or Ronald Reagan with toothpaste smiles dying painlessly and unbloodied for apple pie and the American way of life. In the sixties, what we saw on TV from this war was noisy, chaotic, dirty, scary, bloody, foul, disturbing, tearful, painful, and heartbreaking. Often they showed war as it was happening. They sent the best reporters, who showed us right from the front lines the bullets, the bombs, the wounded, the maimed, the killed in action. Many journalists were killed, too.

Politicians and the leaders of our military learned lessons from the way this war was reported. The American people became very upset when they saw the blood shed by their own sons, fathers, brothers, neighbors, boyfriends, and husbands. Politicians did not like it that young—and older—folks were regularly gathering to protest this war. In my lifetime, never again would the US military let the journalists of the world anywhere close to the front lines. Sanitized versions would now be reported by military big shots or politicians at briefings held in clean, well-lit, air conditioned rooms with comfortable chairs, maps, and chalkboards. These messages were short—you know, brief—briefings.

In the sixties, we witnessed events on TV that changed the reporting of American military involvement in all future wars. That nightly activity we watched was called the Vietnam War. There was so much excellent reporting on this event that most Americans, if they were interested at all, were educated well enough to actually have an informed opinion.

Many of the mothers and fathers and uncles and aunts and older friends of the boys who went off to Vietnam noticed a big difference between that war in Europe and the South Pacific in the forties and the current war in Southeast Asia.

After 1969, with the exception of the "America: love it or leave it" crowd, many Americans had changed their minds and now believed we should not be fighting in Vietnam. Some of the reason for that was a place called My Lai. My Lai was a village, or a group of villages, in an area that had been targeted by the US military: Company C of the Twenty-Third Infantry Division. Specifically, Charlie Company had been ordered to go "clean out" this area of North Vietnamese soldiers and personnel. What occurred on March 16, 1968, would not be made public until 1969. By 1970, it was well known that several platoons of American soldiers had massacred up to five hundred women, children, and old men at My Lai. Many of those killed were marched to a ditch and shot. The military tried to cover it up. Washington tried to cover it up. For this tragedy, only one man would be convicted and sentenced to three and one half years of confinement to a military base. This same man offered his first apology for this terrible event on August 19, 2009, forty-one years later, at a Kiwanis Club luncheon of greater Columbus, Georgia. Three months earlier, I had turned sixty.

There are no excuses for what happened at My Lai. But this man who apologized was more of a sacrificial lamb than anything else. He and his group landed in Vietnam in December of 1967. They were young, like me. They were inexperienced. They went on many patrols and watched one after another of their buddies lose limbs, organs, and lives from stepping on booby traps. While they knew the enemy was there, they never once faced him. The first time they did was when they were sent to My Lai and told that everyone who was still there late in the morning were North Vietnam supporters or military. The South Vietnamese people, these soldiers were told, would already have left the villages and gone to the market that day.

On March 16, 1968, I was in college. Three nights each week, I was a tavern boy serving up and down beer to wild and crazy college guys looking for a good time, and wild and crazy college girls looking for Mr. Right—or Mr. Right Now.

Listen: ending wars we have not won or are not winning is a tricky political moment. Our political leaders must end the bad war that we're losing or should not be in while confirming the good war we've been fighting. They must do this at the same time. They must do this quickly, while taking their time. They must figure out how not to offend the mommies and daddies, the brothers and sisters, the wives and girlfriends and children, the buddies of all those men and women who've already died with their boots on.

In the early sixties, the Vietnam War, like everything on TV, was in black-and-white. By the late sixties, it was in "living color"—dying color, too. Many of us now had color TVs.

The 1968 Democratic National Convention was in Chicago toward the end of August. Robert Kennedy had been killed just eighty days before. Martin Luther King had been killed sixty-five days before him. And now, in broad daylight, on the streets of Chicago near the convention center, the Chicago police were beating up anyone who came to protest that Vietnam War. The police did not discriminate. The word 'gestapo' and fascist was often used to describe their actions. Often the police came out of nowhere and charged unsuspecting demonstrators. Their tactics were brutal: journalists, doctors tending to the wounded, women, young men, anyone in their way. After beating everyone, they dragged them and threw them into paddy-wagons. Hundreds of people were wounded. This was someone's plan. This was 1968 America. This was Mayor Richard J. Daley's doing.

On the convention floor, CBS reporter Dan Rather was pushed, shoved, and belted in the stomach by security guards when he tried to ask a delegate from Georgia why he was being manhandled off the convention floor by other security guards. CBS's beloved evening news reporter, Walter Cronkite, high above in the reporters' booth, was talking to Rather, the rookie reporter, while this event took place. I was watching and listening to Dan and Walter talk to each other. Dan, a thirties Depression baby, was thirty-seven years old. I was nineteen. Mr. Cronkite, a World War I baby, born a year before my mom, was fifty-one years old. Mayor Richard Daley of Chicago, the orchestra leader of this tragedy, was sixty-six, two years older than my father.

Dan and Walter's microphones were on. Dan Rather was punched down to the floor; he was having trouble speaking and breathing. "I'm sorry to be out of breath…but someone belted me in the stomach… we tried to talk to him"—Rather got up off the floor—"to see why… who he was…what the situation was. But the security people put me down. I didn't do very well."

"I think we've got a bunch of thugs there, Dan," said Walter Cronkite.

Mayor Daley was adamant: no crazy young people were going to take over his city. There were many young people there; perhaps thousands of them. No matter, Daley had almost twelve thousand police, seventy-five hundred national guardsmen, seventy-five hundred army troops, and a thousand CIA agents to back him up. Anyone caught making Chicago look bad was going to be badly beaten, even if the TV cameras were rollin'. Young people were there because Abbie Hoffman and Jerry Rubin, the leaders of the YIPPIES (Youth International Party), told them to go; because Bobby Seale, founder of the Black Panthers, told them to go; because Rennie Davis and Tom Hayden, leaders of Students for a Democratic Society (SDS), told them to go. The YIPPIES petitioned the city to hold a convention. The permit was denied, but many came anyway. Mostly they came to protest the Vietnam War.

While Dan Rather was being roughed up inside, thousands were being roughed up outside. Then protest leaders took the students out of the parks onto the streets, so the city itself would be tear-gassed as well as the demonstrators.

In 1968, it was my turn to be nineteen years old. "What the fuck is wrong with you!" I shouted at the TV.

"You sons of bitches… you assholes!" I shouted at the already verbally abused TV. It wasn't just students they were beating. Seventeen reporters were beaten, injured, and arrested. Doctors tending to the beaten were roughed up and arrested.

Listen, I was alone watching it as I ate lunch at home. I stopped eating. I could not eat another bite. I was working that summer in my dad's supermarket because summertime is when you send all your full-time workers on vacation. Let the boy fill in here and there. My dad was sixty-four, and he had been working for over fifty years. But back in 1925, when he was nineteen years old, he was learning the grocery and meat business from his mother. He was learning the Charleston too, but not from his mother. It was a good year. So was 1926 and 1927, and 1928.

And now, in 1968, I was crying, watching something I could not understand. It was brutal; it was a street war. The Chicago police were winning. This would go on for three days and nights.

I was crying and screaming at a TV set. "What the fuck are you doing?" I shouted. "Who do you think you are...you pigs!"

Our black-and-white TV set had recently been replaced with a new color set. I could see the blood on bodies, faces, and hands.

We had an antenna on our roof so we could get half a dozen channels. TV reception was **free**. In 1968, if you wanted to turn it on or off, you had to go right up to the switch on the front of the TV. If you wanted to change the channel, same thing: you had to walk up to the TV and turn the channel changer switch.

Close to the end of the convention, Mayor Daley had his people print and hand out hundreds of signs: DALEY, WE LOVE YOU! Then he staged a pro-Daley demonstration right on the floor the convention.

"Poor Chicago....can you believe this guy?" I said to the TV set. I could not eat a thing. I was upset and felt like crying again, as many of us do when we are young and lose our first love—or our best friend dies in some jungle thousands of miles away from home for reasons we don't understand any more than we understand why the 'she' in our life left us one shocking day.

Riding & Writing

In the summer of 1970, a pretty girl I knew from Baltimore called me up to tell me that the Baltimore police department had just received a grant to replace their motorcycle fleet and were now selling their 1965 Harley-Davidsons. It seems like a strange thing for this young woman to call about, but it wasn't so strange if you knew that I was in love with Harleys and had always wanted one, and that the girl doing the calling thought she was in love with me.

"You bought a what?" my dad said. We were in his grocery store, in one of three back rooms. It was summer, and I was working for him again as I used to do every summer since I was fourteen. I was finally as tall as him. In fact, I think I was a bit taller. I was twenty-one years old. He was sixty-six.

"A motorcycle," I said again. I had bought it a week ago. For the past week, I had been keeping it at a friend's house. I had been trying to figure out how to tell him.

"How did you pay for it?" he asked.

"I had some money, and a friend loaned me the rest, Dad. I bought it from a police department." I hoped the police department reference would help my cause.

"Who did you borrow the money from, and how much did you borrow?" he asked. I told him, and we went out into the back parking lot to see it. Much to my surprise, he wasn't as mad at the idea of the motorcycle as he was about my borrowing the money from a sweetheart from school. He explained that he would give me the money to pay her back, and I would pay him back from my earnings this summer.

"There will be all hell to pay when your mother sees it," he announced. "She will not stop complaining about it until the day you sell it."

JUST RIGHT

My, my, something's coming alright
and it's tasting like a tall tropical suck on the ice cubes drink
I've got my order in

Rock and roll ready for some new spice to mix into my recipe
me in top shape digging my todays
like some space out musician makin' make sense music
working out the rhythms of life
putting it all together now just right
not knowing where it's coming from
not caring where it's going

What a rainbow ride singing tunes day and night
lying down only to make love
and rest my ever lovin' laughin' muscles
no time to get sick
or fat
or ask too many questions

Jesus this feeling is taking over
like coming on in second gear on the meanest badest buggy
that will flip your switch

on a sexy road with the mountains to your left
and the ocean to your right
and absolutely nothing behind you got it all with you now
out there up the road whatever it is
it's got to be you feeling this way
moving at speeds that would shock superman
kissing the face of life and death smack dap on the lips
and then spinning out just in time
to avoid a long lasting relationship who needs it right now
that's all.

Summer of 1970

Banano

THE FOLLOWING YEAR, ON ONE of my trips back to college, I stopped in upper New York State to pick up my motorcycle. I had loaned it to a friend. He had attended Antioch College with me but had recently transferred to a college in New York. I picked it up at his apartment. As payment for the use of my motorcycle, he'd changed the oil. Nice.

It happened on Interstate 70, about thirty miles outside Columbus, Ohio. I was passing a tractor trailer and doing about seventy-five. The speed limit was seventy. As I was about to complete the pass, I lost all power. The motor kept running, but it felt like it was in neutral. The truck I was passing went by me, and fortunately there was no one behind us. I pulled over to the right and slowly came to a stop. When I inspected the bike, I noticed that the drive chain, which turns the rear wheel, was missing. So I walked back down the highway until I saw it stretched out on the road, lying straight as an arrow in the passing lane.

When I picked it up, I saw that it had broken at the master link. The master link holds the chain together. That's when my legs started to shake. The chain did not break; the master link broke. Chains break in many places, but rarely at the master link. Usually when the chain breaks, it wraps itself around the rear tire, causing the bike to stop all forward motion. When this happens, the motorcycle driver generally loses control, falls off, and rolls around on the highway getting hit by other vehicles as he or she bounces along at over fifty miles per hour. Often the driver of the motorcycle breaks bones and damages internal organs; or dies. My legs continued to shake as if they had a mind of their own. "Good grief, I should be dead," I said to the highway and the blue Ohio sky.

My friend who did me the favor of an oil change had not adjusted the oil drip that lubricates the drive chain and keeps it from getting too hot. If it gets too hot, the chain will break. In 1971, Harley-Davidson motorcycle chains that were not properly lubricated almost always broke. Chains break, but I had never heard of a master link breaking. Exactly why I had another master link in my saddle bag I will never know, but it was in there. I stopped shaking shortly after Columbus, where I stopped at a Harley dealer who adjusted the oil drip and tightened the secondary chain to the rear wheel.

"Dude," said the mechanic, "you should be dead. No lie."

Every chance she got, my mother was now giving me kisses on my cheeks and expressing words of joy. I'd recently told her I had sold my Harley. I'd sold it to live out my dream of being Ernest Hemingway. For that, I would need to fly to the Caribbean, get up early, write every day, drink rum often, buy a horse, and live on a beach with a pretty woman. So that's what I did, at least for a little while—actually, longer than I expected.

My plan was for a two-week stay. But one night at a casino in San Juan, I got lucky at a craps table. My two-week stay would evolve into almost three months.

At the table, a stranger said to me, "Hey, you look like you're doing all right." He was older than me. He had on a panama hat and was dressed in a white silk suit that said "money." He did not appear to be the kind of guy who had to sell anything to make a trip down to San Juan to vacation. Having always enjoyed a good hat, I noticed him right away.

"I'm having a good night," I said.

"Jake," he said and held out his hand. "Jake Thompson." I told him my name, and we shook hands. He was an American. I told him it was the first time I had been in a casino. "Whatever I've won, it was more luck than skill," I confessed.

"I don't shoot craps, but I like to watch it," he said. He was a businessman who had an apartment on Luquillo Beach. He described it and the little town it was in. It was way out on the northeast coast of the island. The place sounded heavenly.

"Eight, the hard way," said the stickman. For ninety minutes I mostly won, and then I left the casino before I gave it back to the stickman. I took my winnings, left San Juan, and rented an apartment one block from that white beach in Luquillo. Luquillo had gorgeous white beaches that frequently appear on lists of the prettiest beaches in the world. I rented an apartment, and I bought an old horse from a farmer up in the hills right below the El Yunque rain forests.

The buying of the horse was complicated than I'd expected. The farmer spoke no English. I spoke limited Spanish. "Hola. Como se llama?"

We had taken a 'publico', a public taxi that stopped for us and often others all going in the same direction. It was like an 'Uber' before Ubers were invented. We could not call him. We along with others just waited at a certain spot on the road.

"Banano," said the farmer who owned the horse. I had asked him the horse's name. Banano was for sale. We had already got to that part. The horse's name was Banano because he was the color of a ripe Puerto Rican banana.

"Cuanto cuesta?" I asked. I wanted to know how much money he wanted for the horse. The horse was old, and I bargained with him some and bought him for forty dollars. The price included an old saddle and bridle.

"Cincuenta dolares," he said.

He wanted fifty bucks. I offered him forty. "Senior, cuarenta dolares".

In 1970 POCO played at Antioch College. They played outside, on a gorgeous spring day, on a stage built right on the athletic fields. I was there with a pretty young college student who had curly, silky black hair. She also had a dog, a Lab mix named Friday Night. He had silky, jet-black hair, too. She and the dog were from New York City. She, her older brother, the dog, and her mom lived way up on Amsterdam Avenue, near the G.W. Bridge. She was part Cuban and part Puerto Rican and 100 percent New Yorker. At the moment, she was my girl.

She rode the horse I bought home to our rented house. She rode, I walked.

Just six weeks earlier she was riding something else. She was driving my 1965 full-dressed Harley. I had to sit behind her so I could hold the bike up when she came to a stop. The bike had a gigantic black bicycle seat. Her five-foot-three-inch frame could touch the ground all right, but she was not big enough to hold this monster up. She could drive it just fine, and she looked as good on it as she did riding the horse. Most of the time, she wore blue jeans. So did I; hip-hugging bell-bottoms to accommodate my cowboy boots. Yep, all grown up and still wearing cowboy boots like when I was seven years old, playing with Kathy in the backyards of the houses on Long Hill Road. Cowboy boots: they were my footwear of preference and still are—dark-brown Nocona boots with a medium toe. I guess I have owned five or six pairs of them since the late sixties. I usually keep them for about ten years, regularly putting new soles and heels on them before I break down and buy a new pair.

I would have to start the Harley for her—no electric start in those days. On the left hand grip, you could adjust (retard) the spark; with your right leg, you cranked it to start just like my uncle and my father with that old Model-T truck in 1920. They cranked in 1920. I cranked in 1970. In 1970, if you wanted to ride a motorcycle, you cranked.

It was the fall. We had been in Puerto Rico almost two months in our cottage just one block from the beach. We could afford it because it was hurricane season. People would come to this area to vacation, but not during hurricane season.

I was writing every morning. I was working on my short stories. Each morning before writing, I walked one block to an empty lot where I tied up Banano each night. Early each morning, Banano and I went for our daily ride on the beach. During the ride, he and I would go swimming. He loved it. All the bugs and ticks came off him, as they did not care much for the salt water. After our run and swim, I rubbed him down, brushed him, and then fed him. Then I would go write.

One morning I noticed the size of the waves breaking over some kind of reef two or three hundred feet out from the beach. This part of the beach was a little cove. It was our favorite part of the beach. These waves were gigantic, maybe ten feet high. The night before, a hurricane had blown through about fifty miles to the north. I went back for the pretty girl with the curly black hair.

"She has to see this," I told Banano.

At first, I thought she was waving at me out there on that reef. I waved back. The crashing of the waves made it impossible to hear her. Then I realized she was in trouble. She had been swept out by the undertow. She was now on the other side of the waves, which were crashing often, and she was too frightened to swim through them to return to the beach. Later I would learn she did not swim out there. She was screaming at me to help her. I dove in and went for her, but the big waves tossed me around like I was a leaf in the wind. Everything was getting very bad very quickly. She was still screaming, and I had failed twice to get to her. There was no one around. So I ran around the cove and jumped in the water. I had decided to swim to her from behind the crashing waves. It was a long swim, but I made it.

Exhausted, I grabbed her and headed for the beach through the gigantic waves. There was no way I could go back the way I had come. In a moment, the wave picked us up and threw us down back into the sea. I lost her again. The wave took her. The wave took me. I went down over and over and finally righted myself to begin to swim to the surface. I swam hard. And then I bumped my head on the bottom of the ocean—I had been swimming down, not up. I flipped around, and in another moment, I reached the surface. The pretty girl was nowhere on the surface. Still gasping for breath, I took a big breath and went back down. I found her on the bottom and brought her up to the surface. We were now out of danger, and I brought her in onto the beach. We both had drunk a fair amount of seawater. You know how salt water tastes so awful? When you're drowning, I found out, it doesn't taste so bad. I crawled out of the ocean and pulled her out. She coughed. I pulled her onto the beach. Then she coughed some more. Then she puked. Then I puked.

Two days later, I put her on a plane so she could see her doctor in New York City. The day before, we had waited three hours in an emergency room in a big chaotic hospital in San Juan for a completely unhelpful medical moment.

In a week, I packed up to leave, too. I gave Banano to a young girl we'd befriended on the beach, whose father had said she could have him. Life had turned sour. It goes that way sometimes. For my girl and me, our future was nowhere to be seen. Our moment was past. We couldn't get beyond the big waves. It took me a long time to find the guy who could not swim through the big waves to save the girl with the silky hair in a timely fashion. And she was confused that her young man could not swim quickly enough to bring her back to shore, where the water was not trying to kill her.

Sam Caplan, my grandfather at the turn of the 20th century

Tom Caplan at age eight, 1912

Evelyn Caplan, 1930's

Tom Caplan, late 1930's

L to R...Sherry, me & Donna in the early 1950's

Tom Caplan in the early 1950's

me...Blair Freshman Football, 1963

88 Long Hill Road, 1980's

Caplan's Supermarket, around 1949

Tarn-poker-game, late 1980's

Chris Dick and Ben... poker-game late 1980's

Tommy and Samantha, mid 1990's

Karen and me

Backstage in San Francisco, 1971

BETWEEN 1968 AND 1972, I made many trips to the West Coast. I drove. I hitchhiked. I took a "drive away" (drove someone else's car). I went alone. I went with friends.

In the spring of 1971, some friends who had graduated from Antioch had recently found meaningful work in San Francisco. They were roadies for the band Dr. Hook and the Medicine Show. They were famous for singing the Shel Silverstein song "Cover of the Rolling Stone." Roadies, in case you didn't know, were the young men who set up the show and then broke it down afterward: the lights, the sound equipment, the instruments. They traveled with the bands from concert to concert. This band had a real stage presence because when they performed, they gave new meaning to the word "wasted": not wasted in the sense of used up carelessly, but in the sense of drunk, hammered, smashed, high, intoxicated, fucked up— practically unable to stand up, let alone play great music. Truth is, they never touched much of anything until the show was over.

My buddy Chris from Antioch and I made the trip out west together during the summer of 1972. We were going to visit these friends who were roadies. We were invited to attend the annual Hookers Ball, held at the Cow Palace in downtown San Francisco. The band was playing at this event, and Chris and I enjoyed this show from backstage. Van Morrison performed that night as well. We had the time of our lives, for many different reasons.

In the years to come, one of these roadies grew so good at the trade he became a manager of these show-tours, running Madonna's world tour in the late eighties. Recorded on one of her live albums is her voice screaming his name for help: "John"!

He is in advertising now, doing corporate work in Dayton, Ohio. Can you believe that? He told me in an e-mail several years ago that after twenty-five years of being on the road—as Robbie Robertson of The Band said in the movie *The Last Waltz*—he had to get off the road and away from rock and roll, or it would soon kill him.

In the summer of 1972, the spread backstage for the bands, the crews, and their guests looked like it could feed most any third-world country, and there was enough alcohol to bring about world peace for an entire week. Others close to the band provided entertainment that could be sniffed, shot, swallowed, or smoked.

Music was a gigantic part of the sixties and seventies. During those years I also saw Jimi Hendrix, Joe Cocker, the Grateful Dead, Bruce Springsteen and the E Street Band, the Doors, George Harrison, POCO, Nilsson, and Dylan. Thirty years later, as an old fart, I had a dream of mine come true. My friend Tarn called me up one Sunday afternoon early in the first decade of the twenty-first century and said, "What are you doing?"

"I'm about to cut the grass." In the summer time, it was a weekly duty.

"Get your blue jeans and your boots on, honey! We're going to see the Rolling Stones in Hartford right now!" he yelled into the phone. "I've got the tickets in my hand!"

"Far out!" I yelled back.

New Orleans, winter of 1973

In the early seventies, as my friend and I drove into the city of New Orleans, there was a maniac who was shooting people in the downtown area. In my lifetime, as far as I can remember, this guy was the first to do such a bizarre thing. He must have been a messenger from the future demonstrating to us that soon, angry and confused human beings of *incorrigible behavior and armed conflict* would somewhat regularly be shooting battlefield semiautomatic weapons at unsuspecting human targets—sometimes as young as six years old—and killing them. It would happen all over the country—from sea to shining sea, you might say. What is more remarkable is that no one would do anything about it.

So my friend from college and I drove into town the day this disturbed guy had shot so many people. I was there hoping to work for a newspaper in New Orleans.

The shooter's name was Mark Essex. He was a self-described Black Panther. He was an angry African American man looking to even up the score: recently, the New Orleans Police Department had shot and killed two African Americans. It was New Year's Eve, 1972, when twenty-three-year-old Mark Essex parked his car close to a downtown police department, got out, and killed his first policeman. In spite of his attempt to deliver racial justice, the first policeman he killed was black, a nineteen-year-old rookie just hired by the New Orleans Police

Department. Mark Essex was soon to become a groundbreaking nut. We listened to this story unfold on the radio as we approached the city.

Listen: on January 1, 1863, President Abraham Lincoln declared a presidential order called the Emancipation Proclamation. The order freed all the slaves in the United States. One hundred and ten years later, Mr. Essex declared war on the New Orleans Police Department for what he saw as their failure to honor that presidential order.

On December 31, 1972, Mr. Essex sent a handwritten note to a local TV station. "Africa greets you. On 12/31/72 at 11:00 p.m., the downtown New Orleans Police Department will be attacked."

Seven days later, after shooting twenty-two people and killing five policemen, Mr. Essex was finally cornered. He retreated to the roof of the Howard Johnson Hotel in downtown New Orleans. My college friend Eric and I were just pulling into town. Up on that Howard Johnson roof, Mr. Essex was having a gunfight with a police helicopter and hundreds of policemen. Mr. Essex was finally surrounded. The posse had arrived. The radio announcer told everyone to stay away from the downtown.

It was a modern day Bonnie Parker and Clyde Barrow moment. In 1934, Bonnie and Clyde, the famous bank robbers, were shot to hell and back by police officers with machine guns, rifles, and handguns. Like Bonnie and Clyde, Mr. Essex had over two hundred bullet holes in him when they took him off the roof.

Forty-four years later, in July of 2016, following the precarious unexplained deaths of two more (in recent years there had been a string of suspicious deaths of unarmed black boys and men by white policemen) black men at the hands of white policemen, Micah Johnson, a twenty-five year old black American Afghanistan army veteran, who supported the New Black Panthers Party, declared war on the 2016 Dallas police department and set out to kill white policemen. These policemen were protecting hundreds of black, Latino, and white people who were peacefully demonstrating in reaction to those same deaths of the two black men. Mr. Johnson killed five white police officers; wounded seven white officers, and also wounded two by-standers. Mr. Johnson was killed once cornered in a parking garage. Refusing to surrender, the police sent a robot to him to blow him up. 'Plus ca change, plus c'est la meme change'.

Back in New Orleans forty-four years earlier, Mr. Essex was now a dead twenty-three-year-old. At that moment, I was a twenty-three-year-old, too, but I was alive. I would not get hired by that New Orleans newspaper. Instead, I painted houses with my friend Eric until it was time to go back to Boston and look for the girl who would never marry me when I asked her to, but would always want to when I did not.

A Pine Box

IN THE WINTER OF 1974, I hitchhiked home to Wallingford from the house on Surf Drive on Cape Cod, where my car had been totaled by the mayor's son. I was leaving the girl (again) whom I had often asked to marry me as soon as she no longer wanted to. She still had the dimple in the middle of her chin. She asked me why I was leaving again. I really could not say. She cried, and I held her. I would soon learn she'd had enough.

I was home in Wallingford. My dad, who was in Florida on vacation with my mother and several other couples, had asked me to check on the buildings. I had not been home a week when the call came at around four in the morning.

In 1974, phones did not have caller ID. When you answered, you were often surprised. I felt around the little table by the bed for the lamp's switch.

"Dick, this is Jake Stein. I have some awful news, and there's no easy way to tell you. Your father has died. It looks like he had a heart attack."

"What!" I said. I thought he'd just told me my dad had died. And my mom was not doing well. For a second, I wondered if I was dreaming.

"Your mom will need help getting home," Jake Stein said. "I think you should call your sisters and have one of them fly down here and take her home." My sister Sherry would fly down right away and bring Mom back. She did not have two young children, as our older sister Donna had. Sherry got our mom, and I flew down and brought our dad home. I was twenty-four years old.

At the time, I didn't know I just needed to call Bailey's Funeral Home. It was about one mile from our home. Mr. Bailey would have taken care of everything.

"I'm taking my dad home to Connecticut," I said to the pretty blonde at the TWA check-in counter. "He passed away here in Florida."

"I am so sorry," she said.

"Can you check to see if he is on the plane?" I whispered.

We buried him, as our custom dictates, in a simple pine box. As suddenly as he died, we buried him. Jake Stein called me Monday night. I went down to Florida on Tuesday afternoon. I came back with him on Wednesday. We met with the rabbi on Thursday night. He was buried on Friday, before sundown as custom dictated.

He was seventy years old, and just too nice to die. I thought he'd always be there. He knew so much but told me so little. We didn't have enough fun together. We didn't have enough time together. He worked. He always worked. And then he worked some more.

There were cars everywhere. The funeral home parking lot was beyond overflowing. Cars were parked on both sides of South Elm Street, for as far as one could see. Inside the funeral home, my mom, my sisters and I sat there forever as people passed by and shook our hands, speaking softly with tender words. Everyone knew him. It seemed like all of Wallingford was there. After the funeral on our way to the cemetery, we drove right by his supermarket, and the driver stopped for a moment at the front door. The new owners had closed the store during the funeral services.

During the fifties, when I was old enough, he would take me to the store on Sunday mornings to check on the equipment. In those days, the store was closed on Sundays. We would go down to the basement to check the compressors that ran the dairy, produce, meat, and frozen-food cases. We checked the freezers and coolers. We would go to the office and he would review the past week's sales.

There was no product in the produce cases. Everything was sold or in the cooler. These cases had been washed; so had the deli and meat cases. And in the coolers, there was not much of anything. If you ordered right, you sold almost all your produce, fish, and meat by Saturday afternoon.

You know, I had never gone on a vacation with him. My sisters tell me he was worried about me. He was worried all those women in our home would spoil me. He was right to worry. Once he took me to a baseball game, the second game of the 1957 World Series (the Yankees against the Braves). Whitey Ford, Don Larsen, Yogi Berra, Billy Martin, Hank Bauer, Elston Howard, Tony Kubek, and Mickey Mantle were all on that 1957 New York Yankee team. The Yankees won that game but lost the series.

Now he was dead. I was only twenty-four. At the graveyard, tradition told me to take the shovel. I took it and scooped up a shovelful of dirt from the big mound that lay next to his grave. I dropped the dirt on my father's simple pine coffin. Then I did it again and passed the shovel. I walked a couple of feet away, and I looked up and saw the girl with the bangs, the long brown hair, and the dimple in the middle of her chin. And then I held her and finally cried like a baby.

US 61 and US 49: Clarksdale, Mississippi

IN 1973, MY MOTHER WAS fifty-five. She was recovering from having had a noncancerous tumor the size of a grapefruit removed from the outer part of her brain one year earlier. Years ago, neurologists and psychiatrists had all agreed that the "change of life" was at the root of her headaches and depression, not any biological causes. She had been misdiagnosed for over eight years. "Evelyn, you should see a psychiatrist," said her internist Dr. Horowitz in 1969, not knowing what more to do.

Four years later, in 1973, she experienced a seizure. A month later, she checked herself into a psychiatric evaluation unit in a big-shot teaching hospital in New Haven. There, close to eight years after seeing first her physician, then a neurologist, then a psychiatrist, they found the tumor. A surgeon took it out, and she started to recover.

Ten months later, in March 1974, her husband died one night in a Florida hotel room. He had been sitting on the side of the bed. "Evelyn—" It was the last thing he said to her. Then he fell onto the floor.

If he had been ill, he did not tell anyone. I never knew him to miss more than two days of work, ever. That was back in the midfifties. He had the constitution of a marathon runner and the spirit of the Little Engine that Could. He was larger than life to me; he was larger than life to so many people, especially in his town.

I had no idea what was to come next. I wasn't even sure of yesterday. I didn't even know that Wallingford was not really my town anymore. Ten years had passed since I'd lived here. Two weeks earlier, I couldn't have told you where I wanted to live. But I could certainly have told you I would never want to live in Wallingford ever again.

For many months following his death, people I knew and people I had never met kept stopping me on the street, and in local stores, bars, and restaurants. They had important information to tell me. They had Tom Caplan stories. Tom Caplan stories had something to do with a guy, or a child, or a family, or a friend of the family in some predicament. The stories always had the same feature: (as Gregory Bateson used to say) Tom Caplan was "the difference that made the difference" in some difficult moment of a person's life. Even more charming, no one but the recipient or close family ever knew.

"It was private, like a secret," she whispered to me. She stopped me right on North Main Street. She had been telling me about an incident. I had no idea what the heck she was talking about. She was in her late-forties, and she was telling me a story about when she was a little girl here in town during the late thirties, during the Depression. She was so sincere. She had a great smile, and she was animated as she told me how he had helped her family in a certain way.

"No one else would ever know, but we were so appreciative" she whispered. She was telling me the secret. Private, the stories were always private.

He was my Atticus Finch, of course, the hero of Harper Lee's *To Kill a Mockingbird*. And he was also part George Bailey, son of the banker in the movie *It's a Wonderful Life*. Jimmy Stewart played George Bailey. George sent his younger brother to college. My dad, Tom, sent his younger brother Itzie to college. He sent my sisters, and he sent me too. He always stayed behind.

In 1974, I sent my sisters on their way. I sent my sisters on their way to explore the world, to discover or invent their lives, to leave Wallingford behind and start fresh again. Then I stayed behind. Just like him. It was just like the earth's magnetic field. You couldn't see it, but it pulled me, all right. I wasn't going anywhere.

My mother's surgical incision had been healing nicely, but right after my dad's funeral, the wound had become infected. She was in need of another operation. Her body was rejecting the piece of acrylic the surgeon had put in to replace the part of the skull he had removed to get the tumor the size of a grapefruit out. There was my sister in the Midwest, with the husband and the two young children, and there was my other sister in Boston, all settled in her profession. There was his business, his real estate, his stocks. And there I was with no plan other than a desire to become a famous young writer who traveled. We all agreed after the funeral. We talked.

"Dick, have you thought this out?" my sister Donna asked.

"Of course I have." I was prepared to stay for the long run. I was prepared to stay back in Wallingford. I was prepared to stay in his town and care for our mother.

"Could you be happy here?" Sherry, my other sister, asked.

I was lost in some kind of "son thing," some kind of father-son thing. Whatever it was, it was powerful, but it was clear to me I had to remain. It did not hurt. I was too numb. For the moment, I was all out of ideas.

He left me several pairs of shoes. In a moment, I stepped right in one of those pairs: the take-care-of-your-mother pair. I thought they fit. I thought I should wear them.

"Happy? What do you mean?" I didn't know what they were talking about. I was thinking about what was needed. They were talking about what I wanted. At this particular moment, I was confused by the word "choice." We were speaking two different languages. "What are you talking about?"

Then there was my dad's younger brother. This brother, in his midsixties, was already becoming impaired by Alzheimer's. Soon he would not drive anymore; then one day he no longer came to the office. Then his wife, Ida, placed him in a nursing home. Then he died, too.

As the years passed, I slowly realized it was time to do something more. The buildings and investments were not a full-time job. They could have been had I known anything about business. But I was the guy who wanted to be a fiction writer. All I had to do now was figure out just what that "something next" was—something close to Wallingford so I could take care of my mother. I put away my pencil. I put away my pen. One day I would let myself wonder why, but not now.

My mother had that second operation. It healed, but it took time. She now had an indentation on her forehead where the same surgeon took out the infected acrylic that he had installed to cover her brain in the first operation. One year later, she had a third operation. The medical team took a piece of her rib and filled that indentation on her forehead with it. She recovered from all these surgeries, but she was never really the same. The medical patient did fine. But her once-strong spirit struggled with her post-operative life. Was it the loss of her husband, older age, medications? I never knew. But anxiety, depression, and mild confusion were now a part of her everyday life.

"Where are you going?" she would ask. "When will you be back?" she would say.

"How long can you stay?" she would ask me once I was inside her front door.

1974: It was a miserable year. I left my girl; my dad died and my mother would need more operations and somehow I ended up back in Wallingford. That summer I visited the girl with the dimple on her chin and tried to persuade her to continue our relationship. I took Tess with me, the mother of my first future golden retriever Joshua. Tess was a good friend's dog I often took care of when he traveled.

During the surprise visit, the girl with the dimple made it clear she no longer wanted to see or hear from me ever again. I spoke of marriage; of settling down. She spoke of seeing someone else. I was heartbroken. Soon she would mail me a small package with all my letters to her she had been saving. It felt like she was erasing me from her life. Nineteen seventy four was not turning out at all as I had imagined it might be. I was now sure it was quickly becoming the worst year of my life.

That same summer another Richard was having a troubled year as well. On August 9, 1974 at ten in the morning, this Richard became the first person to resign as president of the United States. He resigned moments before congress prepared to give him the old heave ho, the boot, to impeach him, to put a pink slip in his pay envelope.

temporary solutions to permanent problems

down
> two quick bottles of cheap Friday night wine
> on top of a crystal clear white powder send off
> fueling burnt memories that flame
> the wondering whying wishing was's that
> pour out non-stop
> delivering delicious details of smiling episodes
> that slipped on an icy part
> and put you sideways
> with cross-eyed questions on your tongue.

watch
> a grey Atlantic sunrise
> freshen up last nights exhaust
> wore down drag your ass off with another lady
> that suits your bed but not your head
> and fuck for a moment coming down sleep
> and wake to an Alka-Selter afternoon.

saturday
> sunsets an instant replay
> of a broken field run

sprinting the nonsense
that keeps perfect time with the rhythm
to the song you're living entitled
temporary solutions to permanent problems.

dawn

down time that's got you roped and branded
blue passionless bottles of beer and dizzy drugs
that loosen the noose of pointlessness
with another noose of pointlessness.

so

sunday morning sleepless eyes awake
on the razor edge of confusion
for the millionth time
to witness mornings answers
to the gloomy questions that you let
bully their way into your life
when she left
you left you
fool.

Summer 1974

Breakfast Is an Important Meal

I HAD MADE A FRIEND in town. He ran the Youth Service Bureau for Wallingford, and he was interested in creating an Alternative High School Program. I was, too. I was very interested in alternative education. So against all odds, we put one together. Then he asked me to run it for him. We studied existing programs in New England and put in some new twists. We hired two teachers and negotiated a location within one of the two high schools in town.

It was madness, of course. My notion of *alternative* was to provide a different kind of learning experience open to all students, to all *kinds* of students. The administration's notion was to provide a program only for students who were failing, truant, or challenging authority in a manner that would upset anyone over the age of thirty. In the end, the administration would do the selecting and set the agenda. They referred to them as "at-risk" students. This Alternative Program was not an *alternative* to traditional learning; it was an *alternative* to dropping out.

"Young people with attitude," I said to my friend Ron. "Young people with an edge." Ron was my boss.

I was crazy, of course. If a student in the program missed some school, I would take four or five students from the program to that student's home. They would all pile into my car. I would ask the students to save the truant because life without a high school diploma would be fairly bleak.

"Bleak?" they would ask. "What the hell is bleak?" If a parent was home, I would explain what we were doing; no one kicked us out. Confronted with their peers, often the student who had stayed home came back to school with us.

Sometimes the teachers or I would meet our students at a local breakfast place and have breakfast together. It was a good way to start the day. The administration and other teachers wondered if we were sleeping with the students.

We took field trips everywhere. We kept telling them they were all in this together. We did not tell them solutions to problems; we asked them to come up with solutions to each other's problems. We shared. We believed in them in spite of their acting out. We just would not give up. They liked that. Some of them started to believe. Some of their parents started to believe. It was exhausting work.

We had some successes and some failures too. Most of the other teachers didn't pay much attention. Many were grateful to be rid of these difficult students. Like adults everywhere, they were way too busy reviewing more important issues in life: money, sex, sports, fashion, or politics.

But now, almost forty years later, there still is an Alternative High School Program in Wallingford. School systems often need alternatives; some human beings do, too.

Smith School for Social Work

"Come in," the principal of Lyman Hall High School said. I was slightly nervous. There was no reason to be—he was one of the nicest men in the school system—but the question I wanted to ask him had implications beyond the request.

Two years had passed since we'd begun the alternative high school program. It was the fall, the beginning of another school year. The sun was shining, and there was not a cloud in the sky. His exterior wall was pretty much all glass. His office was flooded with sunshine. "Hey," he said, looking up. "What can I do for you, Dick?"

"I was wondering if you'd write a recommendation for me. It's for graduate school."

I wanted to go to graduate school because I didn't think I knew what I was doing. I had passion. I had motivation. I had good instincts, but I didn't know what I was doing. I had found something to do (other than writing) that suited my soul. Now I needed to get good at it. We'd had too many failures. So I went to graduate school close to Wallingford in order to maintain the business my father had left and stay close to my mother. She needed a son who would pay attention, and I needed to stop having so many students fail.

"Sit down," he said, loosening his tie and smiling. "Tell me more."

Northampton, Massachusetts, is a beautiful place. From Wallingford, it is only about a fifty minute drive north. In the summertime, for eight weeks, Smith School for Social Work lived at Smith College. Smith College lived in Northampton. During the fall, winter and spring, we interned like students in the medical profession. For me it was like Antioch College, a cooperative-style college education—on campus studying for three months, then working for three months, then back to campus to study, and so forth. Some of the work/study semesters were six months long. I loved it. Many did not.

And yes, there were many more women at social work school than men. The dead baseball player in the movie *Field of Dreams* asks, "Is this heaven?" on discovering the baseball field Kevin Costner's character has built for him. At Smith, a similar thought passed through my twenty-nine-year-old mind.

My second-year placement was at Jacobi Hospital in the Bronx. It was connected to the Albert Einstein Medical School. I worked on an inpatient unit and saw some clients in the outpatient department.

They liked me a lot, and my supervisor offered me a job after I graduated at the end of the coming summer. It was a choice position. I thanked them but declined.

No one knew it, but I had other plans. I had a plan that only the son of Tom Caplan could possibly think was a good idea. It was an act of love. It was pure madness.

The Eighties

IN THE NINETEEN EIGHTIES, MIDDLE schools were empty across the United States. Communities were closing them because thousands of young people were worn out from the sixties and had put off having children. Young American men and women had other things on their minds—especially the women. Empowered by college and sometimes graduate school educations, supportive parents, and notions of possibilities, women in America were entering the workplace in droves.

The last time that had happened was in the early forties, when most of the men had gone off to war, leaving their jobs to go fight the good fight and save the world from the bad guys. Women filled the offices, stores, and factories. They built the fighter planes and made the bombs, guns, tires, bullets, uniforms, shoes, ships, tanks, and practically everything else in America. They went to work and didn't demand anything. All they wanted was for their men to come home from this war in one piece. Many men did not.

Twenty years later, in the sixties, the daughters of the women who had worked during the war entered the workforce again in droves. Again, there was a bad war going on, and again, some young men were sent off to it. But it was a small war, not a world war, so many of the men stayed home. This time the women who went to work really wanted to. They thought they would test their recent educations. And eventually, they demanded something called equal rights under the

Dick Caplan

Constitution of the United States. They wanted the grown-up men, their bosses, to stop behaving like adolescent boys. They wanted equal pay for their employment and the right to be hired even if they could make babies. Babies, they thought, would just have to wait. These women were busy obtaining justice, higher educations, equality, and freedom from girdles and bras. Some even stopped shaving their legs and under their arms.

In 1970, my dad sold the supermarket he and his mother had built to two nice young men who knew a thing or two about supermarkets. He sold it because he was tired, I had no interest, and the brother with whom he ran it was struggling with early-onset Alzheimer's.

In the mid-seventies, several years after my dad died, I negotiated with the attorney of his younger brother Itzie to purchase his stock. My dad's older brother who had no stock, had died in 1967. He died in New York City, where he had lived since the late 1930s. Tom had him buried next to their parents. In 1976, Tom's younger brother was now living in a nursing home, but he still knew me, and we could talk of the old days. Then, the sun went down one day while I was visiting, and it got dark. He said good-bye. When the sun came up the next day, he no longer knew who I was.

His attorney and I were trying to reach a fair price for my family to purchase the 40 percent of the real estate, stocks, and bonds Tom Caplan had given this brother so many years earlier. It took three years of negotiating, and like anyone who wants something really badly, I'm sure I overpaid.

"So what"? I said aloud, leaving my lawyer's office after signing the deal. "I did it!"

In 1971, my dad was sixty-seven. He was tired from a lifetime of long hours and hard physical work. Four years earlier, when I was eighteen and he was sixty-three, I had challenged him to an arm-wrestling contest at our kitchen table. He beat me right-handed. Then I remembered I was left-handed. He beat me left-handed, too. I was almost six feet tall and 175 pounds. When I flexed, there was a large round bump on the top of both my upper arms. They were like rocks. I played football, soccer, tennis, basketball, baseball. I had recently worked all summer long busting up a nineteen thirties-era cast-iron furnace in "the building's" basement with a ten-pound sledgehammer; my dad was buying a new one. I was in pretty good shape, but not good enough. My mother had an absolute fit during the arm-wrestling event. Afterward, my dad never said a word about it.

In 1981, on a sunny day with four weeks to go before I received my graduate degree in social work, I bought back that supermarket my dad had sold to those nice men. The lease was up, and we couldn't agree on a new one. They thought they had me over a barrel, as they knew I was about to graduate from graduate school. They knew me all right, but they had no idea. I'd already bought the real estate and the other investments from my uncle. The supermarket was the last piece. What was once gone would come back; I would return it to the family. I would return it to the family for him. I would return it to him. He would like that, I thought. He would give me an "atta-boy!" They did not know the only son of Tom Caplan. I was about to receive my MSW, but I was still searching for another pair of my father's shoes. I stepped into another pair: his supermarket shoes. I was now thirty-two. I thought they would fit.

I was wearing khakis now. No more blue jeans. Well, I still wore blue jeans, just not to work. In thirty years, my son's friends would say I was one of the few men they knew who could wear a pink shirt.

My wife, Karen, gave me the bad news long ago. "I think you're a preppy," she said.

OK, sometimes I do wear loafers without socks; once in a while, I do wear a pink shirt; I always wear a tie to work. I do wear khakis. I wear shirts with button-down collars. I never button the top button of my shirt, even when I wear a tie. I never pull the tie all the way up.

"But Karen," I said thoughtfully, "I wear cowboy boots. I wear *clogs*. What kind of preppy owns a poncho from South America—and *wears* it?"

"Honey, you own a pair of white bucks," she said,

Good grief, I would never say it out loud but I even have saddle shoes. My god, I thought to myself, I have the blue blazer and the gray slacks. Lord, I even have a seersucker suit. I might be a preppy all right, but a weird wild preppy with long hair, a beard and a mustache, who if he had his way, would live in blue jeans, work shirts, boots and always own a Harley-Davidson.

Karen

DURING THE EIGHTIES, I GOT married to a sweet, smart, pretty woman who had been born in Champaign, Illinois and eventually ended up in Connecticut by way of Wisconsin, Florida, California, and Buffalo, New York. She was married to a scientist who brought her to Connecticut (Wesleyan), but it didn't work out. She is a social worker, too. In spite of all the trouble I cause her, she loves me like you would not believe. We got married in the backyard of my parents' home in August of 1983. It took two rabbis: one from the little Wallingford shul founded by my grandfather and some other immigrants in the 1890s, and another rabbi from a reform temple where Karen studied Judaism when she converted. That was her idea, not mine.

A year and a half later, we had a baby girl, Samantha. Karen gave birth at 7:11 in the morning on a snowy, overcast February day. I was not in the room. I preferred to keep the birth thing a mystery. I wasn't interested, not even a little. I vacuum. I do laundry and dishes. I do windows. I mow. I paint. I even do roofs. I don't do births. Sue me.

At home in the kitchen, when no one was around, I made up lyrics and cheers and sang them to Samantha, "The world is a breast, and everyone sucks...be happy!" I chanted, "Two bits, four bits, six bits, a dollar. All for the bosoms, stand up and holler!"

I was thirty-six years old. So was Karen. In seven more years, when we were forty-two, our son was born. When we went to parent-teacher nights to meet his teachers, there were parents there who were fifteen to twenty years younger than we were—teachers, too!

As my dad had when he was a boy, we lived over the store: different location, same idea. It was in *the Building* he'd bought during the Depression. I even set up a private-practice office for us right next to our apartment. I ran the supermarket, managed the real estate, and saw clients in my psychotherapy practice. I was a busy guy. My model, my dad, had worked hard. I wanted to work hard. I wanted to be like him. I wanted to honor him.

It took me eleven years to burn out. I was in his shadow. Eventually it got dark, and I could not find the light switch or the door out. Aside from many other things, I think I needed a brother, too.

A Boomer Prayer

IN THE EIGHTIES, MANY OF us would evolve into yuppies. Yuppiedom wasn't a religion, but here is an example of what yuppies would have prayed for if it were.

Dear God:

Grant us an above-average-paying job with excellent health and dental insurance, a 401k or a pension, four weeks of paid vacation time, twelve sick days each year, four personal days, eight holidays, parents who can afford to fork over the down payment for the house we want, grandparents who will fund our children's college education, life insurance two times our salary, long- and short-term disability, annual bonuses, and of course a partridge in a pear tree. And God, if possible, please let it be in a really interesting place with minimal traffic, low property taxes, and a good school system. Oh, and Lord, if it's at all possible, please let that house be far enough away from our parents so no one will be dropping in unannounced.

Hey, thanks a lot, Lord.

We Have a Name!

FINALLY, MY GENERATION BEGAN HAVING children. Everything changed, as it has for grown-ups of every generation who turn into parents. Oh, those eighties. Many of us made silent deals with the money devils in American capitalism.

No more cocaine. No more free love. No more demonstrating. No more *Laugh-In*. No more Smothers Brothers. No more Archie Bunker. No more Sonny and Cher. No more hitchhiking across the country. No more crashing in friends' apartments. No more *Happy Days*. No more boys with really long hair. No more bell-bottoms. No more miniskirts. The Band played their last concert. No more chance of the Beatles getting back together. No more Lennon, Hendrix, Joplin, Redding, Morrison, Mama Cass. Ugh.

No more JFK. No more asking what we could do for our country. No more Martin Luther King. It was not a service moment. Not by a long shot. Now it was a Ronald Reagan moment. It was a money moment. It was a corporate moment. It was an are-you-better-off-now moment. Except for George Carlin, Richard Pryor, John Belushi, Robin Williams, Steve Martin, and Gilda Radner, it was "grown-up time."

But, finally, we had a name. The inventor of the name was Landon Y. Jones. Eventually, because there were so many of us, he would simply refer to us in his book *Great Expectations and the Baby Boom Generation*.

The Land

In 1983, I started talking to John Wooding, the son of the builder who'd put up our family home on Long Hill Road, about jointly developing our commercial land. His land, his construction company, was right next to the land my father had bought in the center of town to store dry goods he sold in his supermarket.

It was so long ago that most families were still using cloth diapers. One of the first environmental debates in this country was about diapers and the energy it took to clean the cloth ones versus the disposable ones filling our shrinking landfills. It was so long ago that no one had computers or cell phones. It was even before beepers! Now we have cell phones—the Pony Express, Western Union, postcards, telephones, beepers, radios, phonographs, flashlights, calendars, compasses, game shows, and computers all in one. For a culture obsessed with the right now, what could possibly be better? Talk about your great expectations. Soon your phone will turn up your heat, turn on your air conditioning, open your garage door, start your oven.

"My son will graduate next spring with a degree in architecture," Mr. Wooding was telling me in 1984. Mr. Wooding had three children. Soon his teenage daughter would work part-time for me in my supermarket. She would ring a cash register while she attended high school. The Woodings lived down on North Main, about a half mile past the Choate School in the old Yankee neighborhood. My father employed the mothers. I employed their daughters.

"He could design our uptown project," said a proud John Wooding.

"Yikes," I thought. This could be trouble.

I have a newspaper clipping from 1984 announcing that Caplan and Wooding had hired a development consultant to study the use of privately owned and municipal land that housed the town hall and the police department (multiple buildings on Center and North Main Streets). The town had almost doubled its population since the last town hall and police department were built in the early fifties. These buildings were bursting at the seams. They needed new sites. Their current site was adjacent to my family's land in the center of town.

Also in the newspaper was a story about the former Robert Early Middle School. It was one of those middle schools I was telling you about that had closed during the eighties. It was also in the center of town, half a block away from the current town hall site. The town wanted to sell the current town office sites and relocate to a larger space. The story in the newspaper was that the town had formed a study committee to figure out the best use for this empty middle school. Towns and cities are big on study committees.

"John, this is a big project. Your son hasn't even graduated," I said. "Don't you think it would be wise to get a seasoned architect?"

"No, Dick," Mr. Wooding replied, "he's really good."

Walking back to my office, I said, "Yikes." This time, I said it out loud.

Of course, it seemed to make sense for the town to encourage development in the center of town; the local retail community up and down Center and Main Streets was under attack by malls and big-box stores. People were flocking to them to be rushed, pushed, lined up, confused, and ignored. They went there to buy things that would break before their children were out of diapers, whereupon they would return to the same stores to buy the stuff all over again. They loved it. Wallingford's downtown was so empty that little children could now play safely in and on the main downtown commercial streets. The times, they were a-changing. Somewhere, someone named Sam Walton was smiling. Soon he would be doing an Irish jig.

Three years later, I was still at it, pushing the land's development. I didn't know it, but I was on a fool's errand. Mr. Wooding had already backed out of the deal, as I would not accept his son as the architect. The focus had also shifted from a new development to the renovation of the old Robert Early School for a new town hall.

Two Italian bricklayers, a Jewish lawyer, and a Presbyterian Yankee dairy farmer formed a partnership and proposed a simple renovation of the existing town buildings on the site the town was selling and a cheap renovation of the old middle school into a new town hall. One person in their partnership was more connected at town hall than the two slices of bread in a peanut butter and jelly sandwich. My design was different. It included removing those old 1950's structures and replacing them with new buildings that honored the old historic downtown.

When you lose in the beginning, you often lose in the end as well. The two Italian bricklayers, the Jewish lawyer, and the Presbyterian Yankee dairy farmer won. I was all done with my big-shot center-of-town plans for this lifetime.

I Use to be a Chocolate Chip Cookie but now I am a Cigarette Butt

I WAS ABOUT TO ENTER my regular-guy period. I think I caught a case of "adultitis". My hair was combed, my teeth were brushed regularly, and my shirts were clean and pressed. As a regular guy, I coached soccer in the town's youth league. I ran the Wallingford American Cancer Fund campaign for several years. Word got out I was a regular guy, and good grief—I was even asked to serve as a director on non-profit boards. I am not sure who it was participating in these activities. People keep telling me they remember me doing this or that. I served on the Single Parents' Association, on the Red Cross board, and eventually on the Beth Israel Synagogue board. Like my father before me, I became president of the board at the Beth Israel Synagogue.

"Oh shit, did I say president?" Now I raised my voice. "Holy shit! Dick, you don't even believe in religion anymore. How did you keep a straight face?"

"I don't know" I said to myself. Oh, man. I was practicing to be a perfect fish out of water.

So listen, during my fish-out-of-water period, a Jewish friend I went to grade school with died. I heard he had committed suicide. I had not seen him in years. He lived out of town. Of course, I went to the funeral. He was buried in our small Jewish cemetery here in the industrial part of town down by the factory that makes plastic and cancer.

"What the devil is his grave doing back here?" I asked a member of the cemetery committee. The gravesite was way in the back, by the fence. Trees along the fence practically hid the entire grave. No other graves were anywhere nearby. We were standing in the back of the funeral group, preparing to say some prayers. I was thinking that someone had made a terrible mistake.

"We used this site because he committed suicide," the committee member responded. "In an orthodox cemetery, people who commit suicide are not to be buried with others," he instructed me. This burial site was used by the cemetery committee because over four thousand years ago, Jewish people thought that if you took your own life, you had broken god's law and should be buried outside the gates of the cemetery. Perhaps, I thought to myself, over the centuries they'd come up with burying the person on the outer edge of the cemetery as a compromise. And now, maybe forty-five hundred years after these burial regulations had been established, this little cemetery committee was behaving as if the family, who needed no reminders of their loved one's death or its cause, be dealt a punishing reminder every time they visited the gravesite.

His family had wanted him buried next to his dad. I was president of the synagogue, so the family appealed to me to fix this.

"Come on, this is 1986, for crying out loud. We're not an orthodox synagogue anymore. We haven't been one in what, fifty years?" This was my second try. I had attempted to move him the year before. I had failed. But now I had several new board members.

It took me two and a half years, but eventually I got enough votes from members on the board to force the cemetery committee to relocate the grave of my dear old friend.

The years floated by. I ran the supermarket. I do not remember many moments. I simply remember working. It was like swimming laps. If you own one supermarket, even a small one, you work; you swim. Then you swim some more—not fun swimming, work swimming. Basically, you work or you sink. Your store is now open seven days a week, ten to twelve hours each day. I had about forty folks who worked there, many part-time. Certain features drove me nuts. You really needed to be there most of your open hours. Some customers were nice; some were not so nice; some stole from you. Some employees were really nice; some employees stole from you, too. The daily activities of protecting the store from these occurrences were not enjoyable. And finding someone who was stealing meant only one thing: now you had to do something about it.

I did enjoy making ads. On Tuesday nights, after the store closed, Claire paid bills and I made the ads for Thursday's newspaper edition. You should have seen this Thanksgiving ad I put together in 1982. I designed it to look like a five-star restaurant menu; Starters, Soups and Salads, Side Dishes, the Main Event, the Big Finish. But soon this fun stopped as we entered the world of weekly flyers created by our warehouse for ten or fifteen large independent stores here in Connecticut.

Once in a while, things got interesting. Once in a while, things were off-the-wall.

"Know who's across the street?" a customer said as if he was about to share the best-kept town secret ever.

"Who" I asked?

"You won't believe it," he said. "In fact, you better go see for yourself."

I walked up the first aisle, to the front of the store. There were two gigantic picture windows on either side of the front doors that made up our entrance and exit. Outside, on the sidewalk across the street, were six of them. The view was perfect. They were holding signs and walking back and forth seeking people who would beep their horns in approval. They wore white robes like the KKK, but no sheets on their heads. It was not the Ku Klux Klan, but they could have been cousins. It was group that called itself some kind of world church of the creator. They carried signs that advocated for white supremacy and passed out racist literature. And they were across the street from my store.

"Fuckin' A," I said under my breath.

"What in the hell are they doing here?" I wondered. The next thoughts I had involved most of my meat room staff in their blooded aprons holding their bloodied knives. They were to stand behind me while I walked across the street. Starring out the front picture window I continued my fantasy. They were to sort of speak, back me up while I outlined the consequences to these KKK (want-a-be's) what would happen if they did not immediately return to whatever racist, roach infested, rat-hole they had crawled out of. I followed that thought up with wondering if I were to do such a stupid thing: who could I call to bail us all out of jail?

The Nineties

REMEMBER THE NINETIES? NO? RELAX, neither does anyone else. If it wasn't for two incredible athletes—Michael Jordan and Tiger Woods, perhaps the greatest basketball player and golfer ever—we could probably skip the entire ten-year period.

You've probably forgotten, but no one can remember the nineties because we were busy being computerized. No one had time to think about or do anything else. Everyone was trying to figure out how those damn things worked.

The nineties went by so fast that by the year 2000, people in their late fifties were now referred to as the new forty-somethings. If you didn't die during the nineties and you were over fifty years old, in 1999 you were now officially now younger than you had been in 1989. It wouldn't help you much in the future. In less than ten years, if you were over fifty-five and didn't own your own business, were not a politician in Washington, DC, and didn't work part-time at Walmart, you would soon be fired—given an early retirement package, laid off, let go, given the ax, or told to take a long walk off a short pier at high tide. In spite of everyone being almost ten years younger than they actually were, no employer wanted to pay their health insurance anymore. "Hire a thirty-year-old," the business manager would tell those bosses, "and pay half as much for health care costs."

My Little Pony

IN THE EARLY NINETIES, THE economy fell faster than a shooting star. It crashed into the ground. It stopped. It would take a president to fix things, to get the economy going again, to balance the budget. President Bill Clinton balanced the budget. He also got a little nookie on the side. He got caught with his pants down. It wasn't pretty. As far as sex and American presidents go, he was far from the first. Neither, most of us realized, would he be the last.

In 1991, in that impossible falling economy, I had another learning experience. I declared bankruptcy. My ten-to-fifteen-thousand-foot supermarkets were no longer a viable option in the marketplace. Sixty-thousand-foot monsters had come into the valley and made me and my stores irrelevant. I could not see the forest for the trees. I kept putting all my money into fixing the problems. Soon, I ran out of money to put in. Apparently I was the problem; in a manner of speaking, once the train had reached the station, I didn't have the brains to get off. I didn't know what to do.

One night I had the only dream I ever remembered having that I was convinced was not a dream. It was like being in the same room with the person I was dreaming about. It was so real it was in NBC Living Color.

"Dad! You *are* here! Thank god. Boy, am I in a pickle!" I found the one person I thought could get me out of the mess I was in. My god, I was feeling better just talking to him, just standing next to him, just seeing him.

"You won't believe the mess I'm in, Dad," I said. So I told him, and I asked him if he could come and run the supermarkets with me. I watched him. I couldn't take my eyes off him. Someone should have taken my blood pressure while I was sleeping. I'll bet it dropped so significantly I could have made medical history.

My dad thought about it for a bit. "Naaaw," he calmly said, "I'm not interested in supermarkets anymore, Dick."

"My god," I said to myself in this dream, "he's not interested. How could that be?" Then his image faded.

So if you think a colonoscopy is a drag, you really ought to try bankruptcy. That one can really spoil your day. Turns out this was yet another long line I got in during my lifetime. In the early nineties, people in small towns and big cities were closing their stores, no matter what kind of stores they were. For a while there, many friends and I got enough experience packing, relocating, downsizing, and closing our businesses that we could have opened a moving company. In the end, it was mostly an attorney moment. If you can avoid attorneys during the better part of your life, in good times or bad, many will think you are a blessed fellow or lass.

I told my mom I was going bankrupt and probably losing some of her money, too. "I'm not going to make it out of this one, Mom. I'm going to have to shut down the stores." I was practically whispering.

She thought about it for a minute. Then she said to me, "It's good to get these kinds of things out of the way when you're still young, Dick." She was seventy-three when she gave me that advice. In 1991, I was forty-two. Bob Dylan was fifty. John Lennon, if he hadn't been murdered in 1980, would have been fifty-one.

Beverly Donofrio, from Wallingford, Connecticut, had just recently published her soon-to-be-famous book, *Riding in Cars with Boys*. In 1991, she was forty-one years old. In less than a year, her book would become a best-seller. Soon she would be signing her name on the inside cover of her book for people who'd just bought it. "Good for you, Beverly!" I said to myself. While she was signing her name on the inside cover of her book, I was signing my name to pages and pages of bankruptcy documents.

"Do I use today's date?" I sheepishly asked Mr. Sherman, my bankruptcy attorney.

As Beverly was basking in the glory of a successful memoir, I was about to meet the lawyer from the law firm of "I've got your number" in Waterbury, Connecticut. I was to be deposed. The attorney representing the food warehouse I owed money to was to interview me and find out if I had squirreled away thousands of dollars in a Swiss bank account or stuck it somewhere in the Caribbean to avoid paying my debts. She wanted to see if I owned a $25,000 wristwatch or one or two $60,000 Mercedes Benz automobiles. She had no idea that I had put all my cash into my company in an attempt to avoid the very meeting I was about to participate in. Not only did I run the operation incorrectly, I apparently went down in bankruptcy incorrectly, too. Proper bankruptcy etiquette in 1991—and forever—was to hide all the assets you might possess to avoid ending up with nothing afterward.

So there I was, sitting right next to my attorney in a small room on the lower level of the Waterbury, Connecticut municipal courthouse designed to depress anyone over the age of five years old. The room was ten feet by fifteen feet and had a dirty linoleum floor. There was nothing on the pea-green walls. We, my attorney and I, were on one side of a metal table. She, the attorney for the-I've-got-your-number law firm, was on the other side. We sat down. I took out my protection from my pocket. I put it right in front of me on the table. It was to keep me safe. My seven-year-old daughter Samantha had said so.

"It will protect you, Daddy," she had said the night before. She was in her PJs, ready for bed. Her PJs had horses on them. "The mean person cannot hurt you now." It was her favorite My Little Pony, the pink one. It was a tiny pink rubber pony, about four inches tall, with a wonderful long blond mane and tail. It would protect me, all right, even from the mean attorney the Waterbury law firm had sent to interrogate me. She, the Waterbury attorney, took one look at the pony and made her only mistake of the afternoon. She asked me what the pony was for. I told her. Then she melted. At that point, although no one knew it, the interview was over. My daughter was right. What happened during the next seventy-five minutes was now of no particular consequence to anyone, due to the power of a four-inch-high My Little Pony. The attorney who made the mistake just could not keep her eyes off it. My seven-year-old daughter had nailed it.

Paragraph Flashes

IT TOOK ALMOST TWENTY-FIVE YEARS, but I started writing again in
the late nineties. I used to write early in the mornings about important matters that I thought were either cute or timely. In the seventies,
I did this in Puerto Rico, Boston, New Orleans, and on the Cape. But
in Yellow Springs, Ohio, when I started writing in the late sixties, I
did not write early in the mornings. Like any proper twenty-year-old,
if I could sleep till noon, I did. This mostly had to do with a what the
stand-up comedian Shelly Berman used to refer to as "the morning
after the night before." In the late sixties, I only wrote late at night
when I longed for love or sex and had neither.

But some thirty years later, I began experiencing *paragraph
flashes*. Early in the mornings, several days a week, ideas for a paragraph would wake me right up. I would have no choice but to get up
out of bed and write them down before going to work. For instance,
I wrote a series of paragraphs about a different kind of managed care.
Managed care was on my mind. I was working in a hospital.

Did I tell you, after I closed my stores and had my pockets emptied, I went to work at Bristol Hospital in Bristol, Connecticut? That
MSW I had received in 1980 came in handy in the early nineties. The
managed care most of us knew was about health care. In the nineties,
a few money-people noticed just how much money there was in the
health-care business. And then they figured out a way to take a piece

of it. Since it involved tons of money, Wall Street got involved. If you want to steal large amounts of money legally, you have to have Wall Street involved. It was one of the great hustles of our time. Wall Street promised it would not cost us anything. In fact, they said it would *save* fortunes. Exactly who would save these fortunes was never identified. What can be authenticated is that the owners and operators of managed care got—and remain—filthy rich. And as so many politicians and rich people have told us forever, it was for our own good.

My managed-care plan was not for doctors or anyone directly connected to delivering health care. Mine was for attorneys, whom I believed the notion of managed care should have started with. Listen: to be an attorney in America, you only need to figure out how to attract large sums of money. You have to get the money to come to your office for a moment. Once it's there, the money need only pass over your desk. Then you hire people to see it, count it, talk about it on the telephone, and then type up gobs of papers all about it. And before you pass it on to its destination, you take a piece of it. If you do this regularly, you too can be filthy rich without doing much of anything. You need only notice where the money is and how it travels.

So where do you notice it? You need to be a great tracker, like Tonto who rode with the Lone Ranger. Where do you do all this tracking? Why on golf courses, silly, and at lunch at "the club," at cocktail parties, Chamber of Commerce gatherings, the Rotary Club, funerals, and most important, in town halls and state or federal buildings. Not a bad gig. I even thought about the reviewers for such managed care. I needed a group of people who knew the law, had plenty of time on their hands, and could be hired for peanuts. Here is the group of people I came up with: *convicts in prisons.*

The New News

LATE IN THE TWENTIETH CENTURY, some of us who were now a half a century old thought that journalism had taken ill. It started with the TV news programs. The announcers seemed to have lost their balance and the ability to speak calmly and clearly. They were talking silly stuff like stand-up comics. A few were loud, clever, and often misleading. In the past, the truth had always been a real focus for the news. Real reported news had something called *sources*, which confirmed interesting and important stories. But to some of the newer news companies, sources and verification of facts were thought to be the real problems in the industry. Sources, it had been thought, had to be verified, and often there had to be more than one. Clearly, thought the new news-owners, sources had way too much power. Some news owners thought this had to change. In fact, at the end of the twentieth century, the new owners in that industry changed the job description of a source.

It turns out that journalism was not ill. It was just figuring out how to do what everyone else was doing in the '90s: making fast cash. Sources, it was decided, could now say pretty much anything. They did not have to worry about whether **what** they said was right or wrong, up or down, left or right. It was the New News. It made everything so much easier. The New News was not a Walter Cronkite moment. It was more like a Robin Williams moment. The New News was now to include the part of the stories that were not true. For years, that part had been left out of the stories.

People listening to the New News could now make up their own minds as to which part was true and which was not. Americans, you know, are very big on choice.

Many people liked this new kind of journalism. They were not interested in how Walter Cronkite, Edward R. Murrow, or Chet Huntley and David Brinkley might have gathered the news.

It was proposed by a few journalists that the truth had wandered some. While journalist could not say with any certainty what the truth was anymore, they could certainly say that by the end of the twentieth century, there was now the Howard Johnson School of Journalism: the truth along with the news, and reality came in twenty-six flavors.

We might even say that the news industry was entering a new era. This was clearly the age of the commercial; truth and reality, as far as the news went, were irrelevant now.

A Sit-In

In the early 1990s, after I sold some of "the land" to the town, someone with time on his or her hands—probably an attorney in Wallingford—decided to make one of the buildings I sold to the town just like the White House or the Mark Twain House in Connecticut: historic. The town was preparing to take down that eyesore of a building, now known as 390 Center Street, to widen a dangerously narrow little street called Wallace Avenue that led to my back parking lot as well as other land Mr. Wooding and I sold to the town.

Someone had different plans. Someone in Wallingford quietly filed some paperwork, and this building was now untouchable, even by God. This building was now on the National Historic Registry. Somewhere in Washington, DC, in one of hundreds of four-drawer fireproof file cabinets in some gigantic office building, sat a folder in the Wallingford, Connecticut section with "390 Center Street" written on it. The folder was in one of the file cabinets that said "Connecticut" on the outside. On the inside, in alphabetical order listed by towns and cities, were individual folders of all the historic buildings in all these communities in Connecticut.

This recent filing was done to stop the town from taking the building down to widen Wallace Avenue. Without a wider street, no one could develop that land. And sure enough, no one would, for more years than you have fingers and toes. The land sat and sat and sat and sat. You would have thought it was a regular sixties moment. You know—a sit-in.

Someone thought 390 Center Street had great historic importance, even though neither Mark Twain nor the president of the United States had ever slept there. In fact, it was perhaps the ugliest building in all of uptown Wallingford—perhaps in all of Wallingford or even Connecticut. If you were going to build a new four-story brick building, no one in their right mind would bring their architect to 390 Center Street and say, "See that building there? Design me something like that."

Some people in town were wondering if some of the local history buffs had swallowed some pills left over from the sixties and were suffering from a new disease called "historyitis." The history buffs themselves were saying that 390 Center Street had architectural importance.

Many people believe Frank Lloyd Wright to be one of the most important American architects to date. He was a regular Babe Ruth of American architecture. Frank Lloyd Wright died on my birthday, April 9, in 1959. I was ten years old. He was ninety-one. If 390 Center Street had architectural importance, everyone connected to the field of architecture could be confident that Frank Lloyd Wright, in spite of being dead for over thirty years, would not only have turned over in his grave, he'd have danced on it.

A Name Change

In WALLINGFORD, AND EVERYWHERE ELSE, when elected officials want to do something—or nothing—there is only one idea that they will suggest: have another study. One day, a local architect told the Wallingford town council everything they'd previously told him they wanted to hear. And sure enough, before you could say "backroom politics," the town hired the Jonathan Rose Company from New York City to review the Caplan/Wooding town-owned land and write another interesting thirty-page report. The land was back in the news. The sit-in was over. The Town paid $1,428.56 per page to have the Jonathan Rose Company tell them what they wanted to hear.

The Rose report said exactly the same thing the other reports said, except that the Caplan/Wooding land was now referred to as the Wooding/Caplan land.

"Someone somewhere has an idea for this land…" I said aloud. I was talking to myself.

Not Golf Too!

ON MARCH 19, 1966, FIVE young men from Texas Western College (soon to become The University of Texas at El Paso) took the court against the Kentucky Wildcats basketball team in the NCAA men's basketball tournament. Kentucky had won this event four times (1948, 1949, 1951, and 1958) and had appeared in the finals six times. They were a powerhouse. As always, the players were all white. Their fans were waving the Confederate flag.

The Texas team was pretty good, too. They were 23–1 for the previous season. They had never won the NCAA basketball tournament. In fact, no team from Texas had ever won. When the starting five took the floor, some people were surprised. They were all black. Then they won: 72 to 65. Remember those people who were previously surprised? Now they were now really surprised.

Five years later, in 1971, Kentucky recruited its first black basketball player ever. He was seven feet one inch tall.

In 1971, Clifford Roberts said, "At least golf is safe." Clifford Roberts was the cofounder of the Augusta National Golf Course in Augusta, Georgia. The Masters Golf tournament is played there.

This young man was exactly what his parents had named him. He could not lose. White men in pants that, as the comedian Robin Williams said, "not even a respectable pimp would wear" were going nuts with his wins. He was black and after all, this was a white man's game, played on white men's golf courses at white men's country clubs.

My friend Chris asked me long ago, "Want to know the quickest way to lose a personality?"

"How?" I asked.

"Join a country club." Chris has always been a man who knows how to turn a phrase.

Tiger Woods was a nineteen-year-old black athlete in the late nineties. He had recently stolen this game of golf and played it like it was something his family had been doing for generations. Fifty years ago, his kind was not allowed to play on over 99 percent of the golf courses in America. He could caddie, but not play. But there he was, and he only knew how to play one way. He played to win, never to come in second or third. He was so talented and would win big tournaments so fast that one advertising company offered him parts of Europe, the entire state of Mississippi, the South American country of Argentina, and Canada's British Columbia just to wear their clothing when he played.

In the thirties, no one at the Wallingford Country Club—like the rest of the country—ever imagined a black man or even a Jewish person being allowed to join any private country club. During the thirties, Joel Smith was the golf pro at the Wallingford Country Club. He had a buddy he would invite to play golf there. After the eighteenth hole, they'd go into the clubhouse and have 'a few'. That buddy was Tom Caplan.

"You ought to be a member here, Tom," said Joel Smith. He turned to the bartender. "Hey, Frank, give us another round."

"Don't rock the boat, Joel," Tom Caplan told the golf pro.

Tom Caplan knew who he was, where he fit in, and where he believed he did not. Joel did not listen. He rocked the boat. And much to everyone's surprise, Tom Caplan the Jew was voted in.

Toward the end of the nineties, the bad jokes about Tiger being black stopped. Eventually, there just wasn't anything funny about what he was doing. No more sarcastic comments about fried chicken on the menu at the winner's banquet. Soon the watermelon jokes stopped.

"Why?" my ten-year-old son asked me.

"Because excellence isn't funny; winning all the time isn't funny." I told him.

Tiger kept winning everything. He even won the Masters tournament at Augusta National, the extremely white, male private country club in Augusta, Georgia.

"As long as I am alive, all the golfers will be white males and the caddies black," said Clifford Roberts. He was the cofounder and the chairman of the board at Augusta National Golf Course from 1933 to 1976. He died in 1977. Thirteen years later, they let the first black man into the club. The year was 1990; 125 years after the slaves were freed. But the club would still not admit women or let them play on their private golf course.

Augusta National had a real problem in January of 2012. They're very big on tradition at this golf course. They have a tradition that they *always* invite the new president of IBM to join the club. They knew anyone who was the CEO of IBM had to be "the right kind of people." On January 1, 2012, IBM elected a new president and CEO. Her name was Virginia M. Rometty—a woman. And yes, she did play golf, but she would not play at Augusta National. Apparently, she was not the right kind of a woman for Augusta National. But later on in 2012, the club finally elected two women for membership in the club.

Tiger Woods won the Masters in 1997. Then he did it again in 2001, again in 2002, and just for fun again in 2005.

Several years later, Tiger, now married and a father, got caught—like so many presidents of the United States—getting some sex on the side. Not even the 2008 world economy fell as fast as he did when the story broke. "Thank god," said many white people on golf courses across the country, in their checkered pants and orange golf shoes. They were saying this out loud and to themselves all over America.

Saved by His Father, Religion, and the Supreme Court

BY THE LATE SEVENTIES, PART of my generation was all through with peace and love. Many were all through with, "Ask not what your country can do for you, ask what you can do for your country." Now many of us were more interested in "Are you better off now than you were four years ago?"

Young people of the sixties were now busy evolving into the human beings who, at the turn of the twenty-first century, would help elect a president endowed—despite managing to graduate from Yale—with the kind of brains you usually had to go on safari to find. Like most of the baby-boom generation, this future president would spend the sixties partying, drinking, and raising as much hell as could be raised in New Haven, Connecticut, while attending an educational institution that manufactures presidents of the United States just like the Ronzoni Company makes spaghetti.

In the sixties, he was saved by his father, but he was still years away from being saved by religion. He was over thirty years away from being saved by his brother, and then saved one more time by the Supreme Court. In the sixties he was still some thirty-seven years away from what would be his major achievement: he would play a significant role in bringing about world economic collapse early in the twenty-first century. Like all of us, he would have his good days and bad.

Some people say he wasn't really elected president of the United States. Some people say friends of his father and his brother stole it for him.

President "W" Bush, who did not go to Vietnam in the sixties, started two wars during his terms in office. Wait till you find out the reason he took the United States to war against a country called Iraq.

AMA: Against Medical Advice/AMA: American Medical Association

IT TOOK ME TWENTY YEARS to get back to New Haven, but I did get back. I did my first internship there when I was in graduate school in the late seventies. It was where I met Karen, my wife.

In the eighties, after graduate school, I had to try to be a businessman in Wallingford. In the nineties, I returned to social work in Bristol, Connecticut, at Bristol Hospital. Dig this: I worked just blocks away from Oakland Street in Bristol. My wife's father, Harry Stephens, had grown up in a house on Oakland Street some sixty years earlier. I used to walk right by that house while I smoked a cigarette after having my lunch. He was tickled when I told him. Like many people in my lifetime, he said, "It's such a small world, Dick."

I worked on the mental health unit and in the detoxification unit. I worked in the emergency room, in the day-treatment program, and the outpatient counseling center. I even did some outreach. I did this all throughout the nineties, right up until the moment when everyone thought the world would close down because computers did not know the century was changing.

Here is an example of a little outreach I did. We had had a patient who was detoxing from some drug abuse. He left AMA (against medical advice), which in this case meant before his detox was over. Later that same day, he holed up in an empty warehouse with a gun. He was going to kill himself, he told the police. So they sent me and a nurse he'd befriended while on the unit.

This was the second time in my life I had assisted the police because some confused young person holding a gun was considering killing himself. The first time was years earlier, in my private practice. A young man had come to see me because everything in his life was falling apart due to his drug abuse. I spoke to him honestly. I thought he had three choices: jail, death or sobriety. As far as I knew these were the only outcomes I knew that were knocking at his door. Then I told him he could choose.

At one in the morning following the day I evaluated him, I received a call from a police captain in Meriden, the town north of Wallingford. The young man was now in his apartment with a handgun in his lap, threating to commit suicide. The police captain on site informed me that my client had requested my presence. They called. I went. The captain updated me. I decided to ask him if we could sit down with him in his living room. He agreed. We talked. He listened. He talked, and we listened. The night wore on. The captain and I took a break and left the room. I had an idea: order breakfast. Food would help him sober up. We would break bread with him. We ate, and soon he surrendered his gun. Sometimes it goes like that.

After breakfast, we all went outside to let the rising sun shine over us. The boy's father arrived and thanked us. He thanked me a gazillion times. He asked me to send him the bill. He gave me his address. He asked me to send it to him, so I did, but he never paid it.

The young man who went AMA from Bristol Hospital did not kill himself either. Food helped here as well. He ate. We ate. He came out, sat down, and cried.

The Managed-Care Boogie

TED WAS AN ARROGANT, PREPPY-LOOKING therapist who worked in the Bristol Hospital counseling center. He was a handsome fellow who was always reading some textbook during our team meetings on the unit, when we discussed patients. Someone told me he was working on a PhD in psychology. One of his jobs for the hospital was to come to the inpatient unit to find referrals for the outpatient department; these departments did not trust each other, and few psychiatrists would refer patients to them. During the nineties, no one in health care trusted anyone else. During the nineties, the money in health care was shifting to a Wall Street moment: a managed-care moment, a nonmedical moment, a competitive moment.

Listen: I attended an interagency team meeting at the counseling center concerning Shirley, a married, middle-aged woman the inpatient department had transferred to a state hospital weeks ago. She was extremely suicidal and cut herself often; she needed a longer-term inpatient stay than eight weeks in the Bristol hospital. The handsome know-it-all guy led the meeting. This woman was a "career" mental health patient. These folks should really be paid by the medical profession, as they spent most of their lives in psychiatric and psychological health care, training interns, nurses, and new mental health workers. Shirley was unconsciously out to prove that we did not know much of what we were doing. In her case, she had a point.

After a month-long stay in the state hospital, they were getting ready to discharge her. The state hospital thought the day treatment program at Bristol Hospital would be just the thing to stabilize her.

Years ago, day treatment programs were intensive outpatient treatment centers. Clients were driven to a psychiatric center each day and stayed from nine in the morning to two in the afternoon, attending therapeutic groups, smoking lots of cigarettes, eating lunch, and then getting driven home. But insurance companies decided that was too expensive, so accountants stepped in to design a new program that cost less.

Now we have intensive outpatient treatment (IOP) two or three times a week for a couple of hours. No lunch. One day we had the day treatment program (DTP), and the next day we had the IOP. This kind of change happened so often during the nineties that I have named it the "managed care boogie." The accountants were pleased with themselves.

At the meeting, Ted the know-it-all told the state discharge planner that Shirley could come to the day treatment program if she went to live in a halfway house and did not return home to her husband. Ted had decided that her home (her husband) was toxic and not in her best interest. I thought he said she could not attend the day treatment if she did not live in the halfway house. So did all the other people who attended the team meeting. He was deciding where she could live, and with whom, if she was going to get any outpatient treatment.

Ted's decision to select a housing arrangement for Shirley (even if he believed it was in her best interest to avoid marital problems) did not sit right with me; it left the patient with no choice in the matter. The hospital had advised us that they would not release her unless she attended an intensive outpatient program. Good old Ted was practicing for-your-own-good mental health planning, which I found disturbing. So I referred this problem to the hospital's ethics committee.

Remember the newspaper editorial I wrote about the boys stoning the squirrel and the headmaster who thought he was god's gift to the planet? It was another one of those moments. You would have thought I'd been caught participating in child pornography or committing atrocities like those seen in Bosnia or the Congo.

Every day, someone in the hospital administration including the Director of the In and Out Patient Mental Health Department would meet with me to try to convince me to drop the issue. Some of the higher-ups never said, but implied significant negative outcomes could happen. So I called Chris, my best friend. He is a psychiatrist.

"Drop the inquiry," Chris said. "You're right, of course, but that doesn't matter right now. Protect yourself, you idiot." He could call me an idiot because he knew I knew he loved me.

Weeks later, I was in the office of the physician who chaired the ethics committee for the hospital. "Thanks for coming here today, Dick," he said.

He had asked me to come to his office outside of the hospital, about a mile away. He had a friendly face, a nice smile, and a firm handshake. His eyes gave it away. He was sincere. He was honest. He was the real deal. Like my father, he had integrity. He did no harm. "I wanted to talk to you about your recent request to withdraw the ethical concern you raised. You know, this is just the kind of concern that we would love to review. I think we could all learn something here. Why are you withdrawing it?"

I wouldn't tell him why I was withdrawing the problem. I wouldn't tell him someone had kind of threatened me. "Did someone ask you to withdraw it or threaten you?" he asked.

No one was going to beat me up. No one was going to hurt my children, at least not directly. But I needed this job. And I was not interested in being branded a problem. I kept my mouth shut. "Someday," I told him, "I hope we have a chance to review this issue.

But this week is not the time." I couldn't lie, so I thanked him for his concern.

I still felt awful. And I spoke to myself right there, on the sidewalk in front of the doctor's office. I said, "Shame on you, Dick!" At that moment, I decided I would never fold again.

I liked to think I was big on principle; I probably still do. In ten years, that promise to myself would end my career in social service. But it would be OK. It would take me a while, but I would discover that I wasn't entirely different from that know-it-all guy from the Counseling Center. I was pretty full of myself, too, and just as silly.

Children's Games

AT THE END OF THE twentieth century, I was 51 years old. The United States of America was officially 224 years old. We have survived wars with England, with our own Native American populations, with France, Spain, Cuba, and Mexico, with ourselves, with Germany, with Germany again, with Japan, North Korea, Vietnam, Granada, and Iraq. And now we were warring with Afghanistan—and back again with Iraq.

On December 14, 2011, almost nine years after the second Iraq war started, a different president, elected in 2008, oversaw as the last soldier in Iraq boarded a plane with his comrades to leave. That soldier was 20 years old. I was now 62 years old. I was home having a drink of scotch and club soda over ice. In the winter, I enjoy a little scotch, but I can't drink it in the summer. In the summer, I drink a little vodka, my grandfather's drink of choice. Scotch was my father's favorite drink. I was watching the evening news and having some peanuts with my scotch, some cashews with a little sea salt.

There was a special feature of the ending of this war in Iraq, the TV reporter announced. "The same general who ordered the army into Iraq nine years ago is now ordering them out."

This war was like most every other war. The rich profited, the politicians fibbed, many of the poor died, and the middle class paid for it. "If there is any democracy in Iraq or Afghanistan, we will have to send tens of thousands of troops back there to locate it." I told Clio.

In 2003, the forty-third president, who himself never went to war, would make war for the United States of America. For the second time in less than three years, he would start a war. This war was against Iraq, a country that had not attacked us or recently attacked our allies. He told everyone Iraq had "weapons of mass destruction."

Turns out the whole war thing with Iraq in 2003 was a "gotcha," which is when someone gets fooled about something in front of a lot a people. In this case, it was the White House doing the fooling. Some think the president of the United States got fooled by the vice president and by the secretary of defense. Then the president fooled about 290 million of us.

Like the brains living in the White House that some people never could locate, we also never found what had sent us into war in the first place: Iraq's weapons of mass destruction. We looked for years, but we couldn't find them. Not ever. Honest.

In 2003, the president of the United States made history. In spite of graduating from Yale University, that prestigious center of learning, George W. Bush, the son of the forty-first president—also named George—became the first president to declare war on a nation for *not having something that they were not supposed to have.*

In 2003, I was fifty-four years old. George W. Bush was fifty-seven years old. He and I are both "boomers." Saddam Hussein, the leader of Iraq—who was off his rocker—was sixty-six years old. Saddam did not know it, but in a New York minute he would be on a collision course with what many thought was his comeuppance. He was born in 1937, during the Depression. My father was in his late twenties during this time period. In 1929, when the Depression started, my mother was eleven years old.

The forty-third president of the United States named the first chapter of this war with Iraq. He called it "The Shock and Awe Show."

This show was very different than the one I had watched on many nights during the sixties, which had put me in the battles, in the jungles, in the villages, on the front lines. Our soldiers were shot at, and often shot. But in 2003, there was no blood, no torn flesh, no screaming, and no dying. No wounded. No trauma of war. No women or children running and crying. No one asked us to gather rubber or medal or other important manufacturing components. No one asked us to sacrifice or buy US Bonds. In fact, the only message we received from the President of the United States during war time was to go ahead and shop, and then shop some more.

This war reporting showed only taped videos of big Iraqi buildings, bridges, ammunition depots, and trains being blown up by smart bombs shot by war ships and jet fighter planes hundreds miles away from the target. They traveled across oceans and deserts like albatrosses who know how to find their way, homing in on their targets in the dark, in the light, in the clouds. It was our first antiseptic war. We would see no blood, no American soldiers injured or killed. Oh there was blood, there were the injured, and there were plenty who died. You could read about it, but you could no longer see it.

Across the nation, hundreds of thousands of fifteen, sixteen, and seventeen-year-old boys and girls watched the show. Many boys still had pimples, and—like me so many years before—were dreaming of touching a young girl's breast or the inside part of her thigh, or of riding a motorcycle. Many of these boys and girls would eventually enlist in the armed forces. Many were poor, just like in the sixties. Their participation could lead to a college education paid for by the military. For many, it was the only way they could go to college. Others thought this war would be like the mother of all video games.

Our 2003 army was an all-volunteer army: no draft. "No worries," I said to myself. "You're an old fart now." My daughter was eighteen. She was to enter college in the fall. My son was twelve. Years from now, many of us boomers would wonder how long this war would have lasted if there had been a draft.

The enemy in Iraq was quickly decimated. Weeks later, it was said that the war was over. Little did we know that it was far from over; it had not even begun. The enemy was preparing its own shock and awe show. About five minutes after our show ended and our president declared victory, the enemy began sending *human* missiles into crowds in Iraq, stealth human missiles. They were blowing themselves up, along with our troops and with those of their countrymen who belonged to a different sect of Islam. *Human* missiles that walked, talked, and took aim. They were deadly.

"Hey, America," these Iraqis said, just like on TV shows right before the commercial. "Stay tuned!"

Outdated Hot Dogs

COMPETITION IS THE AMERICAN WAY. Young boys who, like Cyndi Lauper "just want to have fun," learn about this when they play Little League baseball. In my town, the less athletic players only play two innings. The more athletic players get to play the entire game; they even play different positions. Often—and I mean often—the coach is the father of one of the more athletic players on the team. My nine-year-old *less* athletic son learned about this competition thing right here in town. One day when he was playing, I got up to take him out of the game. The second inning was over, yet the coach had left him in. It was the start of the third inning. This was not because, while running at full speed, he had made a catch over his shoulder like Willie Mays. Nor had he hit several home runs in one game, like Ted Williams. The coach had left him in because only nine boys on his team had showed up that day. If the coach took him out of the game, they would have to forfeit, which would be baseball suicide.

I was looking forward to explaining to the coach that the two-inning thing was his rule. I was going to be cute and tell him I thought it was in my son's contract. My wife, the wise and gorgeous Karen Caplan, saw that look in my eyes. As I got up, she asked, "Where are you off to?"

"I'm going to take him out of the game." I explained my plan.

"Honey, if you do that, I want you to know," she said sweetly, standing in my way on the bleachers at Harrison Park, "eating moldy rolls and outdated hotdogs will become one of the highlights of your life in the years to come." Then she sat down, cool as a cucumber. She too had a way with words.

Having grown up with two older sisters, I was well aware of the wrath of a serious woman. I sat down. The boy stayed in.

Orlando, Florida

I THINK THE DISNEY SONG writers were right. It *is* a small world. You know, like that house in Bristol, Connecticut I'd walk by on my lunch break.

Listen to this: Karen and I went to a dinner party several months ago and met another couple. The husband knew a teacher I'd had at Blair Academy forty-five years ago. They'd been college roommates, for god's sake. I made a stupid preppy crack about how beautiful the wife of that Blair teacher was to the couple we'd never met. The guy agreed. I'll bet this kind of thing has happened to you, too.

"It's a Small World After All" was written partly in response to the 1962 Cuban Missile Crisis. Robert and Richard Sherman, Disney staff songwriters, composed the song for the Disney exhibit at the 1964 New York World's Fair as a salute to the children of the world.

"So, Davie-boy, how long does it take to get there?" I asked. David lived in Woodside. Woodside was a section of Queens. 'Davie-boy' and I were going to the 1964 World's Fair in Queens, New York. Around here, everyone went. Dave lived in Queens and went to Blair Academy too; we had become great friends. We were both fifteen years old. We took the subway. The World's Fair was only fifteen minutes away from his parents' apartment. We saw everything, including the Disney Pavilion.

And get this: in a few years, 'Davie-boy' would date the pretty girl with the long brown hair and sometimes bangs right before I did. His cousin, who lived in West Hartford, Connecticut, introduced them. She was best friends with David's cousin. A year later, David set me up with that same cousin; we double-dated. That's how I met the girl who would only marry me when I wouldn't ask her and never when I did.

In 1970, when Disney World opened in Orlando, Florida, I saw their new "It's a Small World" exhibit. I took the girl who would never marry me when I asked. We drove all the way from Connecticut in a 1964 Oldsmobile Cutlass convertible. We sang songs all the way there and all the way back. Then we went back to our colleges.

The Iceberg Development

IN 2005, NO ONE KNEW it, but *the land* was about to participate in yet another political drama. I called this one "The Iceberg Development." I named it that because some people suggested that the winner of the recent request for proposals to develop the town-owned Wooding/Caplan land had been chosen for reasons you could not see—below the surface, you might say, like an iceberg. So much of local, state, and federal politics behaves that way. The Titanic was a great and mighty ship that sank in the Atlantic because of an iceberg no one could see; the process of selecting a developer sank almost as fast, in part due to things much more powerful than an iceberg: politics and money.

A referendum was held on the town council's selection of this developer. A referendum is a challenge to a political authority that has made a decision that many people do not agree with. Some people who thought they had smelled an inside deal now forced this referendum. After the town counted the votes, the town council's selected developer had to be unselected. Apparently the smell was too big not to be noticed.

The land, quite comfortable living as an empty lot, would now sit some more. It would practice being an empty lot. I could see it from the parking lot of the old supermarket. It was only forty feet away, on the other side of Wallace Avenue. It had been over twenty-five years since I'd first put together my proposal to develop it.

After the referendum and the de-selection of the developer, I walked into the parking lot behind *the Building* and stared at *the land*. I smiled and said out-loud "My, my…doesn't time fly."

On that day in 2005, if I didn't know any better, I would have sworn on a Bible that *the land* was smiling right back at me.

Connections

DID I TELL YOU THAT I left Bristol Hospital in 1998? Managed care was beginning to feel like that famous scene in one of the first *Star Wars* movies, where all the good guys fell into an enemy's spaceship's garbage collection pit. The walls started moving in, and they couldn't get out. If that wasn't bad enough, then they discovered there was a monster in the pit as well.

From 1999 until 2008, in addition to managing our family's real estate as always, I was working as a clinical and case management director for a social service agency in New Haven called Columbus House. Columbus House primarily worked with homeless people, doing street outreach and running homeless shelters, halfway housing, sober housing, and even a little permanent housing. Columbus House also provided transportation to detox or sobriety programs and case management.

If you were homeless in New Haven, single, and over the age of eighteen, you could go to Columbus House. Emmanuel Baptist Shelter, run by the Emmanuel Baptist Church, also had shelter beds for men.

From November to April, when the weather was life-threatening, the city hired Columbus House to open and operate another shelter for men called the overflow shelter. In the late nineties, like the thirties and many times before, America was *overflowing* with homeless people. There were seventy-five beds in the overflow, but often over a hundred men slept there on difficult nights. Even though it was supposed to close in May, often the overflow shelter stayed open in May, June, and sometimes July.

There were about fifty beds at the old Columbus House on Columbus Avenue. There were about seventy-five at Emmanuel. Soon Columbus House would move to a new, state-of-the-art shelter building on Ella Grasso Boulevard in New Haven. We would have even more beds. Of course, there were many who never came into a shelter. They lived on the streets, in abandoned buildings, underground, or in the few remaining woods left near the city. You could say business was great. You could say it, but it didn't sound right if you did.

If you were a single woman, you could only go to Columbus House. There were sixteen beds there. If you were a woman who had children, you could go to one of two family shelters in the city—providing that your children were under the age of twelve. Actually, most family shelters do not allow families to stay there. Men and young boys thirteen and over must go somewhere else. To complicate matters, young boys under the age of eighteen cannot stay in shelters with their fathers. Young boys between the ages of thirteen and eighteen are fresh out of luck if they're homeless. This is why so many homeless families sleep in their cars (if they still own one) where at least they can still be together.

In 2000, if you were homeless and walked into a homeless shelter in New Haven (any one of them) you would be nuts not to wonder just how anyone who worked in a place that looked like this could possibly be of any help to anyone. Most shelters belonged on the pages of an old Charles Dickens novel. They matched the nightmares the residents were living through. They were funded for failure, and pretty much still are. Success in the homeless business occurs in spite of funding, not because of it.

In a moment of clarity, someone once said that working with homeless people is like trying to herd cats. At that level of existence, rest is key to survival. Unfortunately, if you are homeless, survival requires you to move around a lot. When you have no home, no apartment, no car, and no job, you are required to stay in motion most of the time. There are many reasons for this, but mostly it is because no one knows what to do with you or is comfortable faced with the reality of your predicament.

If you move around a lot and don't have a cell phone, it's difficult to find you. In the world of social services, communication is everything. Cell phones have done more to help homeless people than all of America's mental health and social service agencies combined. Follow-up is everything in social services. Files are made. Files are filed. After sixty or ninety days, unused files are removed. If you are found again, a new file is made. The medical social service professions are big on files. We write everything down, but we don't let anyone see it. This isn't kindergarten, you know. We do not share.

If you don't love the work, it can feel like pushing a wheelbarrow full of bowling balls up a steep hill in a cold rain—with a flat tire. My staff would complain from time to time. It was difficult for them to network. Housing, employment, mental health, and substance abuse professionals rarely wanted to collaborate with them. They were paid peanuts. Most of the staff had no more than a high school diploma. Some didn't have those.

These shelter case managers were mostly from the neighborhood. Some were in recovery. Some had been to prison. Some had had relatives shot and killed on the streets of New Haven. Some had been homeless. Many had worked themselves up from being residential monitoring staff in the shelters. They had street experience we needed. They had life experience we needed. When you're reaching out to the homeless, it's best to come at them with authentic people who know what they are talking about. Unfortunately, most professionals do not know. After graduate school, if professionals want to work with the poor or the homeless, they need to be trained by people who come from the neighborhoods where life is fragile, justice is often like a distant relative, and money is a moment-to-moment problem. If they want to be effective, they will pay attention to their coworkers who come from the neighborhoods of the people they are trying to help. They need to learn the things they do not teach you in college or graduate school: college and graduate school does not teach you about "the street."

These case managers were black, Hispanic, and a few were white. Two had college degrees. It was a diverse group, and it grew over the years, as Columbus House won grants and contracts. A couple of case managers grew to five coordinators and fifteen case managers. Most had no higher education, but they had the kind of hearts and street smarts to face what might lurk in abandoned buildings and behind parked cars in difficult neighborhoods. Once they got competent, I told them: "Stop complaining. What are you thinking? You dress like you just came from a drug deal. How do you expect those nice young suburban white professionals to act?"

Next day the coordinators showed up dressed to mingle with young white professionals: shirts and ties for the men, skirts and blouses for the women. Soon after, all the case managers started to dress up for network meetings. On days they were on outreach, they dressed for the street. These folks were learning to be movers and shakers. I taught them the back doors as well as the front doors to the world of change, social service, mental health, and substance abuse treatment. They taught me the street—the rules, the regulations, the procedures. I taught them about connections. It's all about connections.

"It works like Wall Street," I said. "It's not what you know, it's who you know." I made it my business to know everyone at every agency that could help the homeless. The case managers had attitude. I had attitude. Like good businessmen and businesswomen everywhere, we fostered connections.

Some of the homeless are hiding, lost in addictions, family trauma, unresolved mental health issues, and medical problems. Or they're newly released from prison. Some have experienced more bad luck than any life can handle. Most homeless people are hardy, soulful, and spirited. They face significant odds to rebalancing their lives. The residential staff was required to write out incident reports if something happened in the shelter. Something was almost always happening in the shelter. On May 20, 2006, at 5:45 a.m., the incident report said: "Female floor: water broke, client having a baby, called 911."

I loved the work. "It's the most fun you can have with your pants on," I told my buddy Chris in 2001. "Please, no sainthood for me. Just some single malt scotch in the winter."

Just like the famous Green Bay football coach Vince Lombardi did, I created a diagram. I mapped out all the New Haven agencies and how they could move someone out of homelessness into citizenship. I called it "the play." Then I bought some chalk and a blackboard and showed my case managers the play just like they do in the locker rooms. I wore my New England Patriots sweatshirt. We worked on how to block, how to pass, how to run from homelessness to citizenship. Here is how the play looked in 2004:

The Play

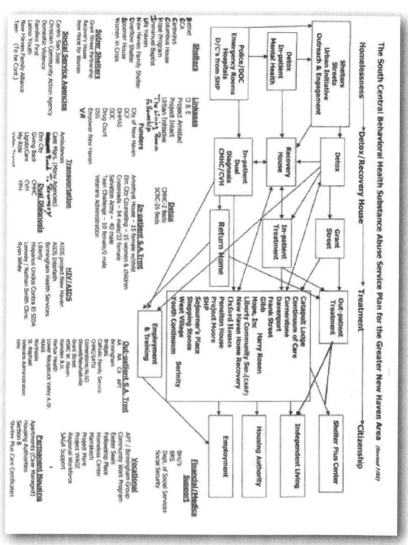

Language Problems, Hearing Problems

AT COLUMBUS HOUSE, WE HAD been working with lots of newly released prisoner in their twenties. Perhaps in anticipation of his own felony conviction for actions unbecoming a governor, and before he was known to the Department of Correction as #15623-014, Connecticut governor John Roland set aside $1 million of funding to design programs that would reduce the recidivism rate of newly released prisoners. Half was for Hartford, and half was for New Haven. Connecticut did have state-run agencies that were supposed to be doing this work, but their success rate was slightly below that of the Jamaican Olympic bobsled team. Prisoners from around the state were regularly released and brought to their hometown or city with less planning than it took to boil eggs. Once they were released on the streets of the streets of the cities of Connecticut, and right after the eggs boiled, they were routinely returned to prison for noncompliance with parole or probation requirements.

Unlike the Wall Street bankers and the investment men who knowingly stole and lost billions and crashed the world economy, young black and Hispanic men in poor neighborhoods across America were arrested so fast you would have thought the police were on a cash-bonus system. In New Haven, the streets were populated by drug runners, drug dealers, and enough crooked policemen to field a new softball league called Easy Money, or Hard Time. Years passed before gunfire was not heard regularly in many neighborhoods. And more years passed before anyone did anything about the police problem. New Haven needed a Frank Serpico.

They were in their twenties, these new bad boys, but they were "street old." The average lifespan of these young boys in the tough New Haven neighborhoods was twenty-five. Funeral homes were flourishing. New gangs were everywhere. Old gangs were everywhere. Crooked cops were everywhere. No more catechisms, bar mitzvahs, or high school graduation parties. Prison was the new rite of passage. Big parties were thrown when you came out. If you kept your mouth shut, you were "the man."

Many of these young men had been the crack-epidemic babies of the eighties. They had difficult childhoods. Crack will do bad things to people, even mommies. It will do even worse things to babies born to addicted mothers.

Over 75 percent of these young men will go back to prison within a year or two. Here was the problem: the system speaks a language no one could understand—parole. Even worse, the young men who were supposed to listen had hearing problems. They could not hear what the white men and women from the DOC's probation and parole departments were saying. So, as often happens when people cannot understand others, they simply stop listening.

The state hired a couple of social service agencies to help. In New Haven, one was run by that ex-Black Panther who went to jail for murder for a couple of years and then took some courses at Harvard University. He was now the executive director of an agency that contracted with the state department of Corrections to house and run programs for convicted men in the New Haven area. The other agency was Columbus House, where I worked with the homeless, the dually diagnosed, the unfortunate, the drug addicted, the unemployed, the underemployed, the unlucky, and those who generally did not have a pot to pee in.

$37,692.00 per hour... at forty hours per week—
oh wait, that's not the paycheck: you still have
to multiply that number times forty hours.

I DID WELL IN THE eighties, operating two supermarkets and a real
estate company as well as seeing clients in a small private ther-
apy practice. Karen worked full-time until the birth of our children the birth of our daughter. She had a private practice and did
Hospice work; then our son came. Since then she worked mostly
with chronically or terminally ill patients and families, with a few
private psychotherapy and coaching clients. We were never rich,
but always comfortable. We bought my old family home from my
mother and put money away for our children's college education.
Everything changed in the 1990's. I spent those ten years digging myself and my real estate company out from more red ink
then a Wall Street bank in 2008. Occasionally, we planned for
our own retirement. We came up short on most fronts, especially
in our ability to save, but we managed to live a comfortable life
and could almost tolerate the stresses of an unknown economic
future once we hit our fifties and sixties. The long term plan was
simple. It was a *Finding Nemo* moment: just keep working, just
keep working......
   Unbeknownst to us and most everyone else, most of the money
in the United States was being reallocated during the eighties, the

nineties, and the early twenty-first century. It has been reported that from 2009 to 2013, over 90% of new income went to the top 1% of the already filthy rich here in America.

In the twenty-first century, there were about 314 million American citizens. If everyone in America could fit on a big boat, and you asked the richest *seventy* families (maybe three or four hundred folks) to move to the starboard (right) side of the ship and then asked the poorest 280 million of us to move to the port (left), the weight of the wealth on the side of the seventy families would capsize the boat. The other 280 million of us (that's 90 percent!) just do not have enough collective bucks to right the ship.

Larry started his company. It was very successful. Then he took it public. Larry earned $78 million in 2013. He was the CEO. Yep, he earned $37,692 per hour before benefits. What did he do? His company sells computer hardware and software, database management systems. The guy's company sells organizational information and storage facilities. Larry's a great communicator. He organizes his time well. He is a mover and a shaker. He also has incredible folks working for him. In 2015 the top four people including him collectively earned over two hundred million dollars. So listen: think we could find one or two people who might do this same job for $30 million a year? How about $20 million or even $10 million? So here is the new $64,000 question: do the four of them make over $200 million because no one else on the planet is qualified, or if there are others, because they won't do it for less?

Dennis earned $124,000 in 2013. He earned much more when he worked overtime. One year, he earned almost $145,400. Not bad.

He won't be earning anything anymore. On his last day on the job, one April day in 2014, he was burned to death in a fire. He was trying to save someone. It was his job. He was at work as a New York City policeman. Dennis was one of those evil union people the newly formed English beverage (tea) party would like to stop overpaying and funding. When he died trying to save someone, he was earning $59.61 per hour.

April 15, 1947, Ebbets Field, and January 20, 2009, Washington, DC

THE FIRST AFRICAN AMERICAN PRESIDENT was elected in November 2008, 143 years after the end of slavery here in the United States. He took office on January 20, 2009. His name was Barack Obama. I voted for him twice. Twenty minutes after he was inaugurated, many white people here in the United States were already blaming him for everything from clogged toilets, lost luggage, parking tickets, and high gasoline prices to darkness at night. Of course he was elected; the previous white administration left us in a never- ending war and $1 trillion debt.

In January of 2009, Washington, DC, came to an immediate and complete stop. Politics hit a bump in the road and government was taking a break from democracy. Governing was to be put aside in favor of something some of us thought looked, tasted, and smelled a lot like making *the first black president look bad, weak, and inadequate.* The Republican congress told us they were going to be the *party* of no to the president, of nuh-uh, of not a chance, of I don't think so, of not now, of it ain't gonna happen, of we are not going to compromise, negotiate, dialogue anything with you no matter what you come up with anymore-or--ever-again until you leave.

Most people won't say it, but those years sure looked a lot like April 15, 1947—you remember, the day Jackie Robinson took the field to play some baseball in Brooklyn, New York. Jackie, the first black baseball player to play in the major leagues had just gone out to his position in Ebbets Field, Brooklyn. He was playing for the Brooklyn Dodgers. They were playing the Boston Braves. He was going to play first base so he was good and close to the stands. There would be no problem hearing the comments many white people wanted to share with him. One week later the Dodgers would be playing Philadelphia. More people had similar words they needed to say to him.

"Hey, ni**er, get out of here ni**er." "Ni**er, you don't belong here. Go pick some cotton, ni**er" "Go eat some watermelon, ni**er." said white people in the stands as well as many white Philadelphia players standing on the top step of their dugout including the white coach of the Philadelphia Phillies.

Now in Washington D.C. and many other places, sixty-two years after Jackie took the field, it certainly appeared that many white politicians were still stuck in that 1947 moment. On January 20, 2009, many congressmen and women decided they were not going to play ball with that black fellow, that black man the people of the United States had elected president. They were going to show him, all right. "Go ahead and suggest something, anything," many white congressmen and women said. Their skin was white but their party was red. Then these red congressmen and women announced they were going to become the 'party of **no**'. Then they said, "This isn't racism, it's just politics".

Plus ca change, plus c'est la meme chose.

When this African-American president took office in 2009, he was forty-seven years old. In two months, I would be sixty years old. When Jackie Robinson took the field for the Brooklyn Dodgers that first time on April 15, 1947, he was twenty-eight years old. My dad was forty-three years old. Martin Luther King was eighteen years old, and he had recently decided to train to be a minister.

It would take a long time for Philadelphia, the city of Brotherly Love, to apologize for the fans, the players, and the coach who had called Jackie Robinson a ni**er over and over again on April 22, 1947. It would take sixty-nine years. Jackie would be dead, but the city of Philadelphia officially apologized to him in the spring of 2016.

2016: Good-bye *E Pluribus Unum*

ONE DAY I WOKE AND thought I had something important to say to Hispanic people. Being full of myself was not a part time job for me. Here was my thought: "Hispanic people of the United States, I want to tell you something. I want to tell you what I believe is the path to your success here in America. It's simple but practically impossible. Here it is: You have to stick together with other Hispanic peoples and other peoples of color. You have to stick together even if back in the old country, different groups did not get along. Here in America, Puerto Ricans have to get along with Mexicans. Ecuadorians have to figure out how to get along with people from Peru. You have to realize that here in America, you are all in this together, even those of you who practice different religions—*especially* those of you who practice different religions. Your power is in the size of your group, the Hispanic group. And power (real or potential) is the only thing rich white guys pay attention to ever. And they have plenty of it. They are scared of you just like their forebears were scared of all those Chinese, European, Irish, and Russian immigrants in the mid- to-late nineteenth and early-twentieth centuries. Some of those immigrants figured this out. Many did not.

"You all have to stick together. I know. Sorry to be the bearer of such impossible news."

To tell you the truth, I thought in the twentieth first century that we would all be a much-improved version of ourselves by now. By now, I thought, I would be an improved version of me. Back in the nineties, I foolishly thought that, what with computers and all, the beginning of the twenty-first century would be like the beginning of a new Renaissance. In 1998, I told everybody, "You wait. We are in for another Renaissance."

I thought we would all be a lot less religious and much more spiritual.

I thought people would come before profits a little more. Profits might be important, but now taxes would be fairer. We all would pay our fair share—yes, even the rich people.

I thought the Guantanamo Bay Detention Camp would have closed quickly due to so many people demonstrating against it. I thought the rule of law would not have been put in the broom closet in the White House. I actually even thought gun control would be a no-brainer, at least as far as keeping automatic guns and howitzers from the general public went.

I thought we would all enjoy sex even more, but not at the expense of others. We would tolerate men in loving relationships with other men and women in loving relationships with other women. Actually, that's one we did make progress on. We would tolerate different religions— or no religion. And for crying out loud, we would stop slaughtering people in God's name. We would stop trying to control or manipulate women in the name of some god. We would figure out how to be more conscious of racism. We might realize it would never disappear in our lifetimes, but we could figure out how to be more aware of it.

I even thought we might insist on what most of us have always known to be true: corporations are not people; they are a business tool. Corporations have no soul. They do not give a 'rats-ass' what happens to human beings. They have no morality; no compassion; no sense of right or wrong. They do not experience love. They are designed to make and manage money only; usually at the expense of other people not connected to them.

Recently, the highest court in America made has arranged how money can buy democracy on most any day of the week, month of the year, minute of the day. Did they think we would not notice?

I thought we would be better with each other by now. You know, more tolerant, less judgmental. More smiles, fewer frowns. I thought more people might be more interested in—say—someone like the Dalai Lama. People like the Dalai Lama do not do well in America. I think if the Dalai Lama wanted to do well here in America, his people would have to figure out how someone could make a buck from what he knows. Right now, the guy has nothing to offer but world peace, human stability, compassion, kindness, tolerance, and reduced anxiety. In America, how can anyone make a buck off that stuff without the use of mood stabilizers and very big guns?

Maybe not enough people know him, I thought. Maybe the first step should be to get the General Mills Company to put him on a box of Wheaties. We could tell them to say he is 100 percent natural. Organic, too!

"You should try him," we would advise. "He's delicious!"

In 2000, I went to my friend Tarn's wedding. He was getting married for the second time. Many people were doing this. Their first marriages had not worked out nearly as well as they had hoped. Tarn was marrying someone who had been married twice before. In fact, there was an entire industry built around American humans leaving their first and second marriages. My own wife, Karen, was married once before. My best buddy Chris's wife was married before. My friend Rick, the painter, was divorced. My sister Sherry's husband was married once before. One of my best friends, Ben, was divorced and remarried.

At Tarn's second wedding, I was to give a toast to the couple. I was the best man. I gave them my dreams for the human race. I got some of it from the Dalai Lama. I read somewhere that someone had asked him what his religion was. "Kindness," he said. I liked that. I told that story, and then I told the happy couple to remember to always treat each other with kindness. And then I told them that because we're not perfect, we should always forgive each other. Kindness and forgiveness, that's what I told them on that day. That's my dream for *beings of incorrigible behaviors and armed conflict*. For me, too!

My As-if Problem

So let's talk. Let's talk nice. A moment ago it was 1962, and it was all so new for me. I was, one could say, at the starting line. Old people told me how fast it would go. Older people told me I wouldn't believe it, but soon, if I was lucky, I would turn around and be sixty-two, seventy-two, eighty-two, or maybe even ninety-two. They were right. I didn't believe them.

Listen: I haven't told you, but I always had an attraction to the blues, acoustic and electric. Sometimes it's clean and crisp; sometimes it's loud, fast, and full of distress. Other times it has surrendered, and it's soft like a pleasant memory and open like a golden linen blouse that invites young men in to touch or kiss young breasts on warm summer nights. Sometimes it cries like it's a lost child or a grown-up who has lost a lover; sometimes it's like a quiet moan trying to cover up a cry. Sometimes it's a sound that needs some arms to comfort it and free up the tears of distress. I like it all. Everything from Lead Belly to Howling Wolf, Robert Johnson, Billy Holiday, Mississippi John Hurt, Eartha Kit, Aretha Franklin, Blind Willie Nelson, and B.B. King. Everything from Eric Clapton to Keith Richards, the Allman Brothers, Whitney Huston, and Bonnie Raitt, right on down to the youngster from England, Adele.

Did I tell you I play the acoustic guitar? It's a sweet old Yamaha I bought in the late seventies. I play a little and sing some Dylan, some old blues, some folk. I play mostly for myself.

I think this music is authentic. It's the sounds of suffering. All human beings suffer. And did you know you can reduce that suffering simply by playing or sometimes just listening to the blues? Honestly now, do you know *anyone* who has never had the blues?

I haven't said it, but music has been huge in my life at practically every moment; the playing of it as well as the listening of it. The Rock and Roll of the sixties and the seventies always felt like a best friend. It continues to bring a smile or an 'easy feeling'. It understood me. It explained me. I have lived many of those lyrics. I have longed for it all along the way well into my own sixties. It befriended me when women left me as a young man; it comforted me when I could not sleep or find love or when I lost my footing. It kept me going when life proved difficult. It put rhythm in my life when I could not find answers. It put its arm around me when there were none others to hold me; it offered me explanations about impossible situations or when the shit of it all overwhelmed me; it sent me messages of joy, of celebration, of 'you can do this'. It sent me more messages about the how or the why or the why not of it all. It brought me syncopation and sent signals to my brain that sent signals to my hips and my feet and my arms. It said, "GET UP RIGHT NOW AND MOVE!!!!" It helped me interrupt space with love, with movement. It helped me connect with others; kiss others; share with others; hold others; be with others. I t made me get up out of my chair and move with others at dances, in concert halls, at weddings, alone at home, or sometimes I just clapped or snapped my fingers.

I was living the music. I was breathing the music. I was the midnight rider, I had a peaceful easy feeling, I knew everyday people, I gave peace a chance, I stood at the crossroads, I did take it easy, I did think the times they were a-changin', I did dance to the music, I wanted to be a street fightin' man, I sat on that dock by the bay, I looked for a bridge over troubled waters, I have slept with honky-tonk women, I was feeling alright, I was runnin' on empty, and I was convinced I was born to run, I had 'good lovin', I knew a girl from the north country, on the golf course across the street from our home on Long Hill Road in 1972, running naked in the moon light I was the midnight rambler and jumpin' jack flash at the same time; I have heard the sounds of silence, someone did light my fire; often I couldn't get any satisfaction but I got a little help from my friends, and someone did have a piece of my heart but I found shelter; I was not born on the bayou but I did keep on chooglin'; I was there when she came in through the bathroom window; I did have a spoonful; and it was just a shot away; I have been up on Cripple Creek and I have said isn't it a pity; I have wished we could all come together, I have felt that hard rain that was gonna fall, and I knew Mr. Tambourine Man, and on and on and on......

Thirty to forty years later, old musical styles found me. Get this: often I was in the mood for and soon could not get enough of my dad's and mom's music: Jimmy Durante, or Glenn Miller, Ella Fitzgerald, Frank Sinatra, Tommy Dorsey, Louis Armstrong, or Benny Goodman. I found Broadway again in West Side Story and Fiddler on the Roof, Cats, All That Jazz. I broaden my view and delighted in rediscovering the Andrew sisters, Gene Krupa, George Gershwin, and Dave Brubeck. I wanted to hear old movie scores again: Dr. Zhivago, Mary Poppins, early James Bond movies, The Sting, The Graduate, Butch Cassidy and the Sundance Kid.

For the moment, I am well into my sixties. According to the hippies of the nineteen sixties, I am over thirty-five years beyond the age of being trusted. In spite of my age, I never lost the knack of annoying people in authority. Years ago, before I left Columbus House at the end of 2007, I pissed off some big shots at Connecticut's Department of Correction: the parole and probation people. They demanded to my boss that I be brought up on charges of excessive misuse of kindness and compassion. Actually, they found me impossible to work with. I was honored.

So at the risk of alienating myself from perhaps half of my generation and lord knows how many others, I have found myself thinking and feeling the following. It's as if someone turned a switch in some part of my brain that dishes up my very own notions of something called *certainty* and something else called *convictions*. These two notions have apparently gotten together and come up with a way to take me right back to when I was five years old.

When I was five years old and convinced I needed a new toy that had been denied me, I would have a temper tantrum. My mom would say "No, Dick, not now," or "No, Dick, I don't have any money." I was fresh out of luck; I was up the creek; I was up to my neck in doo-doo. I would scream. I would fall down and pound the floor. I would cry like I'd been hit by a bus. This occurred at the drug store, the grocery store, the corner store, and outside on the parade route street corner… I had a severe temper tantrum. I am not sure when I stopped having them, but now, after at least fifty-five temper tantrum free years, they have mysteriously come back.

Here are my sixty year old temper tantrums: I don't cry and scream, or fall to the ground and kick my legs. But apparently I have never lost the capacity to be fully and gloriously, impossibly, and verbally obnoxious. Right or wrong, the ability to keep my mouth shut on certain matters (mostly political) I perceive as an assault on my *certainty* or my *convictions* has somehow retuned to me like the unwanted ten pound weight gain following the year-long diet and exercise program.

Listen: I have not cared for plenty of folks before, but rarely have I ever felt contempt for anyone. Richard Nixon? OK, I admit I felt some contempt for him. Many of us did. We were young. We all believed he knew exactly what he was doing. And Mayor Daley: the mayor of Chicago who purposely sent out storm- troopers and cops to surround us and charge us and beat us up. Sure, I had some contempt for him, too.

But then there is George W. Bush. Another privileged, rich, enti-tled Ivy League upper-class white guy who, as president of the United States, displayed little use for contemplation, no need for perspective, no desire to foster insight or intelligence, and an inability to utilize self-reflection except perhaps in the limited use of ritual prayer. He could not read character any better than he could pronounce "nuclear" or display integrity. As president, he made multiple decisions that affected the well-being of millions and millions of Americans in a catastrophic way.

Here is how I think he operates on a daily basis. Someone con-vinced him early on in life that it really did not matter what you thought, did, or what you do as long as you had a buck to back it up—a buck, and some god to go with it. With that knowledge, he set out to make his way in the world. Who cannot call him successful? When we knew him, he was on his way. You know, I could forgive him for all the trouble he caused our country: how he left us broke, $1 trillion in debt, and entered us into several tragic never ending religious-oil-based wars. I could. But how can you not feel at least an itsy bitsy piece of contempt for a fellow whose only support of so many who had so little of everything came only at the benefit of a few others who already had so much more than they would ever need for ten lifetimes?

And now, still unable to put a lid on my new older-guy temper tantrums, I and many others of my generation have noticed that a certain old journalistic reality we found reassuring—we called it "the news"—has been hijacked and altered to fit some other kind of political and social agenda. It sounds as if what so many of us knew to be true and honest delivered to the average family living in this democracy is now perceived by some of us living in that same democracy to be the black plague; the kiss of death; the Ebola virus of words; the end of free choice; the final blow to economy; the death of capitalism; the end of freedom; the sin of murder; a bad hair day; the balloon that got away; the dropped ice cream cone; the shoelace that snaps; the drip, drip, drip of a leaky faucet; a clogged toilet; and a broken garbage disposal.

Can you dig that? And if that's not enough, then there is Donald Trump; but that's for another day.

7

Forever

MANY PAGES AGO, I WONDERED whether I'd gotten the life I needed or the one I wanted. Of course, I have no idea. Karen thinks it's not a very good question—perhaps not even one worth asking. Karen is practicing to be Buddhist and has a point. They won't tell you this, but pretty much whenever you talk to Buddhists, they always have points.

In the spring of 2011, we got another golden retriever. The previous two goldens we had were boys. I got my first golden, Joshua, in 1978—before my wife, and before children. I had him for a little over eleven years. Then there was Spenser. Like Josh, he would take day trips around the neighborhood. I would have to get in my car and drive around for an hour or so to find them. Fearful of them getting hit by cars, they would and did drive me even crazier than I already was. Once found, they would jump into the back seat of my car as if they were glad I stopped by.

"Oh, there you are" they would say. "So, where have you been?" they would add wagging their tails. "Did you bring the biscuits?"

Running

MARCH 26, 1904 GAVE ME two presents: the birth of my father, and the birth of Joseph Campbell. To be honest here, we do not really know what day my dad was born on; he had no birth certificate. His driver's license said March 26, 1904. On his state of Connecticut health card, it said March 22, and on his death certificate, it said he was born on March 24.

Joseph Campbell was a mythologist, teacher, and writer. Wikipedia says he was born on March 26, 1904. He taught at Sarah Lawrence College in Yonkers, New York. He studied and lectured and wrote books about the stuff that makes us who we are—not the biology or the chemistry part, but the spiritual part, the soul of us. My dad and Mr. Campbell were perhaps born on the same day in the same year. I have this fantasy that had they known each other, they would have admired each other greatly for who they were and what each accomplished in life. My dad would have admired Joe for his intellectual achievements, and Joe would have admired my dad for his love of community and his business vision. They both loved and respected the peoples of the world.

Mr. Campbell wrote about an interesting notion called "following your bliss." He wrote, "If you follow your bliss, you put yourself on a kind of track that has been there all the while, waiting for you, and the life you ought to be living is the one you are living. Wherever you are…if you are following your bliss, you are enjoying that refreshment, that life within you, all the time."

So did I tell you I run? As a young man in my late twenties, I ran three miles several days each week. Of course, I smoked then. I would actually have a cigarette after the run. In the summertime, I'd have a cigarette and a beer. Somewhere in my forties, life got too complicated, and I stopped running. I was practicing a different kind of running: life-running, children-running, work-running, errands-running, fixing-the-house running, or cutting-grass running,—making-ends-meet-running.

My daughter got me real running again. In 2009, I was in New York to see her run in the New York City Marathon. She trained hard and did great. She inspired me; so did those lead African runners. As I watched those lead runners run down the avenues with such incredible speed, grace, and beauty, I practically cried. In spite of almost being an old man, I imagined myself running with that kind of grace. Within days, I decided to make running part of my present and my future—part of my bliss. I worked up to running four miles every other day. Sometimes, if my daughter was around, I would run with her. About a month after I started running, I stopped smoking. For years I had tried to stop smoking. For years I had failed. And then, as Forest Gump would say, "for no particular reason," I just stopped.

Truckin'

WHEN MY FIRST DOG, JOSHUA, died, I did not want another dog. I told everyone I did not want another one. "No more dogs dying in my arms," I told Karen. "I mean it."

Joshua did die in my arms. I would not have had it any other way. But years after he died, Karen and our children surprised me one night with Spenser. It took about thirty seconds, but I fell in love all over again. He was eight months old when we got him; another gorgeous reddish golden. Once he grew up, you never saw a golden that could run so fast. He ran like a greyhound on cocaine. And he died too soon some twelve years later, and once again our hearts were broken. We took him to the vet to have a peaceful painless death. He was miserable. He did not die in my arms. My children were there, and so was Karen. I had to leave because of man-stupidity. I was about to cry in front of my children, so I left. I waited outside, muffled my verbal sadness, and dropped my tears in the woods next to my vet's office.

"I don't want another dog." I said, not knowing what I did want.

Years passed. Many years passed. And then, in the spring of 2011, Karen and the children (not children anymore) brought home Clio. She is a girl golden. She is very different. She wasn't a puppy. She was two years old. The boy goldens were those gorgeous reddish ones. Clio is a golden golden. She's a "papered" golden, a regular blueblood. Her father's name is Tanglewood; her mom's name was Puttin' on the

Ritz. Her own formal name is Northern Lights. We actually have a registration certificate. I'll tell you one thing: she did not need any silly registration certificate to wiggle her way into my heart.

She's a roller, all right—a rock and roller. She loves to roll on her back on the ground. First she has to find just the right spot, and then she rolls. Nine times out of ten, she dips that right shoulder in the perfect spot she has found with her nose and begins the roll. Having rolled one way, she rocks right back the other way. She rolls, but first she does a little move on her back like she was doing that old dance in the early twenties, the shimmy. On her back, she stretches her legs out when she does this move. I swear she thinks she's a flapper. Then, after she is done rolling, she gets up and shimmies in place like she's dancing to that Otis Redding song "Shake." Then she goes twenty feet, and when her nose finds another perfect spot, she dips her right shoulder and does it all over again. In the winter, the snow doesn't slow her down one bit. She makes dog angels. And just like me when I was a boy, she eats snow. I ate snow. We all ate snow.

As well as being a rock and roller, she scooches, too! When she is on her back, rockin' and rollin', she digs her back legs into the ground and then pushes off, scooching on the grass. If she's on a hill and there is a little morning dew or frost or snow on the ground, she can go twenty feet on her back in no time, switching back and forth, left-to-right scooching, using her rear legs to push off as she moves herself down the hill.

We have plenty of room to romp around because of that golf course across the street, or at least we do in the late fall, winter, and very early spring. In the summer, we can go out there, but only right after sunrise or after dusk. The crazy golfers start play about one hour after first light and continue right up until the dark settles on the course.

When the spirit moves her, Clio does a great wolf imitation. She drops her head down, but not too close to the ground—like when she is sniffing for possible edible delicacies. She loves goose poop. During her wolf imitation, she changes her gait and begins a slow, dedicated trot. Her legs now move with singular purpose, and she is careful to keep her tail out straight as an arrow. I ask her, "Clio, are you practicing for a movie role?"

Now get this: in the early spring of 2014, Clio and I have been joined by a third party for our walks on that golf course. We have a new walking partner. Actually, not a walking partner; we have a flying partner. Kaah Kaah Charlie joins us almost every time we step outside the door. He is a crow, a bird. I am inclined to believe that Kaah Kaah Charlie recently purchased this golf course—or at least believes he has full ownership of it. He and his gang patrol this area as if they were defending the Alamo. He flies circles around us as Clio and I walk up and down his fairways. Clio chases tennis balls. Charlie chases Clio and me. He talks to us constantly when he is in sight. I always answer him.

"How are you doing today?" I ask good old Charlie. I am looking up as I talk to him. I often wave to him, too.

"You're looking good up there, Charlie," I tell him, "What's that, Charlie?" I say as I cup my hand behind my ear."

"Kaah, kaah, kaaaaah," he says at twilight and again in the early morning hours. First I hear him, and then I see him. I know its Charlie because of his tail. When he flies, Charlie has one feather that points down and is out of alignment with all the other tail feathers. I don't know why that tail feather points down. I tell Clio, "I hope it isn't too painful."

He is there within minutes of Clio and my crossing the street to walk on the golf course. It's like he has some kind of electronic monitoring system pointed at our front door. As soon as we hit the golf course, he's right there, kaah, kaah, kaahing, flying circles around us. Then the three of us go off on our walk. Sometimes Kaah Kaah Charlie will bring family or his "pack." But it's Charlie who always leads the way.

"You're doing a great job up there, Charlie," I tell him. "We feel so safe with you around."

Occasionally he does not see us. Then I call to him.

"Kaah, kaah, kaaaah," I call. "Where are you, Charlie?" If I give him a moment, he'll come, sometimes alone and sometimes with other crows. He will come right over and circle us.

"Hey, Charlie," I say. "Look, Clio, its Charlie!"

Listen: did I tell you Clio and I have our own open-air chapel on that old golf course. Up the hill by the club house, just below the parking lot and running parallel all along the seventeenth and eighteenth-hole fairways are nine of the sweetest birch trees you will ever experience. They are mixed in with pines and smaller evergreens and some other trees I do not know the names of. Some of them separate the seventeenth fairway from the eighteenth fairway.

One of these birches up next to the parking lot is our own sacred place. It stands about eighty feet tall and is formed by a threesome (three fat off-white-bark-curling and peeling birch trunks) all joined (I imagine) below the earth to support the eighty feet above. I think this birch tree is pretending to be a sequoia tree. At sunrise and sunset, the light moving through this tree becomes a spiritual moment. "Clio," I tell her, "I feel like a wise old Navajo Indian celebrating and honoring nature, the world, or the gods who gifted this landscape to us."

You should see those wispy branches at sunrise or sunset. It's like a prayer. I have given these moments a name: contentment. It is pure contentment. In all seasons, our sacred place droops tons of long, lazy, skinny branches. In the wind they appear to be praying—or, as Jews might call it, "davening," swaying back and forth. With or without leaves, the light at these times catches the branches in mystical moments that whispers to the quiet, the hush, the magical, and invites peace upon us all. On both sides of our birch tree holy-place are two snow-flake trees. The correct names I believe are Japanese dogwood trees. In May and most of June, all the branches support multiple groupings of four of the whitest spade shaped pedals that surround the branches and collectively, from a distance, looks just like freshly fallen snow.

Here I am again on my golf course. I am on my father's golf course. He played golf here. I played cowboys and Indians. I played pretend. Under that sacred birch tree, I am usually overwhelmed with a silly notion. Often I am compelled to say that old Sioux or Navaho or Cherokee phrase, "It's a good day to die." Depending what tribe is speaking, the phrase is thought to be said as: O-pa-hey, or Ho-ka-hey or Yet-ta-Hey. Of course none of these words actually means 'it's a good day to die', but there are a lot of white people who like to think so. Anyway for a moment I am eight years old again. I go ahead and pretend once more and say it in Indian too.

"Opahey", I tell Clio in my best Indian voice. Here is what I am thinking and feeling: *contentment*.

Now, Clio has many pleasures in life other than pleasing me. For instance, she loves chasing tennis balls when we go on walks on the golf course. Chasing balls is a fairly common trait among retrievers. It's her attitude about going on walks that I mostly wanted to tell you about. That's what I have to share with you here. It's a message for you. It's a message from me, or maybe it's a message from the universe via Dick Caplan. It's my hello and my good-bye.

Here it is: "Sometimes there's a ball, and sometimes there isn't," Clio says. "That's life!"

Hey, keep on truckin'. I'll catch you down the road.

The end...for the moment.

EPILOGUE

For generations upon generations across America, across the world, children, young people and adults who live in small towns are often known and referred to as someone's relative. Here in America, it's not part of one's official name as in some countries or in days of old. It's more a conversational reference point. I cannot tell you how many times someone would stop me and say, "Aren't you Tom Caplan's boy?" Or "Aren't you Evelyn Caplan's son?"

"Why yes I am." I would say always surprised someone I did not know knew me. Then they would tell me a Tom Caplan or an Evelyn Caplan story. Even as an adult I was stopped often and asked. Then, of course came: the-tell, the story.

In elementary school, I was my sisters' younger brother. They did not even bother to say Donna or Sherry Caplan; just the girls' "younger brother...."

After I grew up and had children, for a while there I got, "Aren't you Samantha's dad?"

"Why yes I am." I would respond. Then of course I would get the" *wonderful* business" Or "She's so this..." Or "she's so that....." they would tell me.

"Thank-you" I would say.

Then in a moment later I began hearing "Aren't you Tommy Caplan's father?"

As known first as Tom Caplan's son, the phrase always sounded strange to me but I would tell them, "Why yes I am". Then they would need to tell me about how Nice my son was". Or "What a pleasure it was to have him in class". Or "over someone's home" I would tell them, "My son has great friends", attempting to complement their children too.

Ten years ago, when my wife was president of the Wallingford Library Board, I heard "Aren't you Karen Caplan's husband?"

"Why yes I am" I told everyone. Then they would tell me, "What a fabulous job she is doing." Or "She's a great speaker you know" they would say with enthusiasm.

For most of my life I was unsure of many things, but never of my identity.

Plus ca change, plus c'est la meme chose.

It's been some fifty years since a lot of this country was up in arms. Fifty years ago this country was divided with so much bitterness that one side was employing the following phrase in defense of their position: 'America, Love it or Leave it'. The people who said this were not interested in negotiation, in discussion, in compromise. Things were pretty weird back then.

Things are pretty weird these days too. I should write about it, but not today. From 1966 up until my dad's death in 1974, America was a nation divided. People of color were seeking civil rights; young men and women were protesting the Vietnam War; women were seeking equal opportunities and pay in the work place, and medical rights to their own bodies. Gay and lesbian men and women were to begin seeking pride in being sexually different instead of shame.

Now here we are some fifty plus years later and everything seems so familiar to me. It's just as Yogi Berra said: "It's Deja vu all over again." My dad was in his early to late sixties as America burned and struggled in the 1960's. So now forty to fifty years later, as I live through my own sixties, America has come unglued again with issues so similar it makes the hair on the back of my neck stand up.

What can I say? Today, as always, we still have a ways to go with this democracy stuff, this experiment. For now, I simply wish us all peace. I wish all of us on our spaceship called Earth to be safe and to find peace. If it seems elusive, I would remind you of what John Lennon said. In fact you do not even have to believe it; you just have to "Give peace a chance".

ABOUT THE AUTHOR

Dick Caplan spent more than twenty years working in mental health and social service settings and over thirty years in private practice. He is also an entrepreneur and businessman.

Caplan graduated from Antioch College in 1972 and Smith School for Social Work in 1980.

Caplan lives in Wallingford, Connecticut, with his wife, Karen; son, Tom; and golden retriever, Clio. *The Boomer Blues* is his first book.

40618902R00158

Made in the USA
Middletown, DE
17 February 2017